ALEKSANDR MIKHAILOVICH
DOBROLUBOV

ALEKSANDR MIKHAILOVICH DOBROLUBOV

RUSSIA'S MYSTIC PILGRIM

Including an English Translation of:

FROM THE INVISIBLE BOOK

Daniel H. Shubin

ISBN 978-0-9662757-7-3
Copyright 2014
Daniel H. Shubin

Email: peacechurch @ jps.net

TABLE OF CONTENTS

ALEKSANDR MIKHAILOVICH DOBROLUBOV

(TRANSLATIONS FROM THE RUSSIAN)

INTRODUCTION

Brother Alexander, as A.M. Dobrolubov was referred to by his adherents, companions and associates, was the successor to a long line of wanderers or pilgrims in Russia's history. Such people abandoned their secular associates, means of income, permanent home, family, and obligation to the state, and departed into society totally dependant on the charity of benevolent and compassionate people. Their goal was the heavenly kingdom or Kingdom of God, and the means to attain this was by a literal observance of Jesus Christ's words, Sell all that you have, give to the poor and you will have treasure in heaven, and follow me. Matt 19:21 and Luke 12:33. This was the straight way through the narrow gate into the city, and there were few that find it. Matt 7:14.

The travel along this path was also a means of self-perfection. It was time a of contemplation, a time to evaluate a person's priorities and purpose, a time of reflection on the past, and plenty of time to determine the future, if the future was even part of the pilgrim's agenda. Reflecting on the past brought sins and life's mistakes into the present, to allow personal confession to God in the open vastness of the wilderness or desert, and repentance and cleansing of the soul. All of this was to instill a sense of individual lack of God's expectations and the motivation to fill that void with a life of asceticism or the deprivation of secular joys, abstention or fasting, celibacy, and destitution. Blessed are you poor for yours is the Kingdom of God. Luke 6:20. This was moral self-perfection, Christian self-realization, and the attainment of holiness.

Living the Holy Spirit, walking and thinking in the Holy Spirit, every day and in every activity, this was Aleksandr Dobrolubov.

Their goal was to institute a divine kingdom in Russia, without war, without violence, but to be centered on a sincere concern for the welfare of each other. This was Dobrolubov's gospel: the life in the Holy Spirit. By having the heavenly kingdom as our goal, we will set aside sin in our life, we will live in holiness, we will terminate war and violence, our life is the success and prosperity of our brethren and friends and associates. God is everything and all there is, and to apply that to daily living in the harsh environment of Russia, was the purpose of Dobrolubov. Be filled with the Holy Spirit and live the life of heaven on earth.

Although he preached a mystic Christianity, Dobrolubov emphasized the necessary of manual labor. The 2 went hand in hand with each other. And this was the essence of his convictions, cooperative effort for the benefit of the society.

The important part and the reason for Dobrolubov's memory is that he accomplished what he decided to do and very successfully. He did not forget about his early life of depravity and drugs, and his method of atonement was in entering the homes of others and leading them toward the God that he rejected in his youth, and leading them away from the devil that he adhered to in his youth.

The comments of those who remembered Dobrolubov during his eternal pilgrimages compared him to St Francis of Assisi, who traditionally had a covenant with nature. For others, Dobrolubov was the Russian embodiment of John Bunyan's *The Pilgrims Progress*, he was Christian in his life journey to defeat sin and enter God's kingdom. Dobrolubov's *From the Invisible Book* has a consistent form of poetic composition that is similar to David's Psalms and the akafists of Russian Orthodoxy.

From another aspect, Dobrolubov was a sectarian. His essential convictions paralleled those of Molokans, Dukhabors, New Israel, and the many other rationalist Christian communities who were Bible-based as well as separate from the official church and from the state. These groups rejected the icons, rites, traditions, attire, priesthood and monasticism of Russian Orthodoxy. Their services were held in a plain room with only the Bible and perhaps some holy writings of their preceptors. Their ceremony was simple and focused on a study of the Bible and its interpretation in a spiritual or allegorical manner, all of it to bring a person close to God, and to separate him from the evils of the world. Their separation from the state consisted in their rejection of militarism.

Much like the religious philosophy of Leo Tolstoy, these sectarian groups were pacifist; they refused oaths of allegiance and military service. Their theology was likewise simple and even perhaps shallow, but it was replaced by a love among themselves that consisted in the high morality and ethic of their religious community. It was a religion of conduct and ethos, with less theology and ritualism. As noted below in his Biography, Dobrolubov became an adamant pacifist and assisted others of his community to also have this conviction.

Dobrolubov saw Orthodox ritualism and theology as an impediment to direct communion with God, and so he circulated among the sectarians for his inspiration, learned what he could and combined it with his experiences of visions and spirit-filled mysticism. Dobrolubov was convinced that the Orthodox Church with its theology and rites only suppressed the advancement of Christian spirituality, and he rejected the Orthodox religion as an institution.

This was the evolution of his gospel. Although the primary codification of his convictions are in his book, *From the Invisible Book*, subsequent to this, he has no further compositions, except meager letters, and he even rejected the necessary of books. He taught that study of Christian theology and religious interpretation was necessary as a fundamental introduction to the existence of a higher or more aspiring knowledge of deity, but once a person develops or ascends to this capacity of direct communion with God, for a person to be always in the Holy Spirit, then printed books have served their purpose and the only book needed is the Invisible Book, which is the residence of the Holy Spirit in a person and its inspiration. As a result, Dobrolubov walked and talked and lived the Holy Spirit, and was willing to share this with every person he could, to have them acquire the divine kingdom in the present.

Dobrolubov was unforgotten among other poets and writers of Russian symbolism because of his early association with men of Russian literary renown, and his correspondence with them continued through the end of his life. Such men were Valeri Brusov, Andrei Bely and Dmitri Merezhkovski, and Ivan Konevskoi in his early years, all of them part of the symbolist movement of Russian literature.

His ability to create a religious community based on his precepts also contributed to his memory. They called themselves Dobrolubovtzi, and were scattered over the central Volga River valley and into Siberia. But they consisted of few adherents and did not last long. After Dobrolubov's departure to other parts to spread his gospel of Christian mysticism, these groups disbanded and assimilated into other sectarian denominations.

His memory continues to the present because of the depth of his divine poetry, his visions and revelations on the Holy Spirit life.

There is no mention anywhere in Dobrolubov's own writings or any of his biographies of his ever marrying or having a family. This likewise was typical of the individual pilgrims of the era.

This translation of *From the Invisible Book*, as well as his letters, is from the original Russian by the author.

THE RUSSIAN WANDERERS

The most popular of those in this class of Russian wanderers was the Christian humanist nomad Grigori Skovoroda. The final period of his life – from 1769 to his death in 1794 – was his period of mendicancy, an ascetic severance from all the normal comforts of human continuance and also his teaching career. Skovoroda at age 46 transformed himself into a nomad, without possessions and entirely dependant on the will of God, meaning, the kindness and hospitality of Ukrainian and Russian villagers. He traveled on foot through Ukraine and southern Russia, preaching his version of Christian humanism, and writing fables, songs, and philosophic narratives, in the intervals at his various temporary residences.

The concept of wandering as a means of attaining holiness was further developed in the religious philosophy of the Russian Stranniki (Wanderers), which began about the beginning of the 19th century.

The Stranniki were an offshoot of the Russian Orthodox Staro-Veri (Old Believers), and they evolved as the pinnacle of anti-establishment religious thought The life of these religious pilgrims – or pious nomads as they should be termed – was an aimless migration from town to town throughout Russia. They were enveloped in apocalyptical concepts of various types, none of which had any consistency or rationale. The Stranniki had a reputation as an unstable and disorganized dispersal of holy vagrants, while others passed themselves off as fools for Christ. The general population tended to view them as irresponsible. To become a Strannik was a way for a serf to escape the estate of his feudal landlord. Other Stranniki were wanted criminals, and were traveling one step ahead of the police. Hospitality, a customary trait of the Russian rural society, included kindness to Stranniki, allowing them temporary shelter, a place to sleep, food, and provisions to continue on to the next village. The hospitality of Russian peasants towards Stranniki included the harboring of fugitives from justice. The Stranniki entering a typical Russian rural village that day might be an individual, a married or cohabitating couple, an entire family, or several disconnected people traveling in a group.

But because not every person who agreed with this concept was able to sell his possessions, or leave them behind, and begin an aimless trek crisscrossing Russia, a dual level of membership or participation evolved. Many, if not most, of the adherents of these concepts were landed, but they were Stranniki in heart. They would vicariously fulfill the role of a Wanderer by providing hospitality to the genuine Stranniki who would pass through their village. Sympathetic villagers would assist them, likewise hoping for the same reward from God, just as Christ said, Whoever receives a righteous man, because he is a righteous man, will receive the reward of a righteous man, Matt 10:41. Up to the conclusion of the 19th century, landed Stranniki offered asylum to traveling Stranniki regularly, while the newly arrived would propagate their tenets in the homes that welcomed them. Towns and villages had orphanages for children of such Stranniki couples.

Modernization in Russian at the beginning of the 20th century caused the demise of the Stranniki. All of them were eventually assimilated, one way or another, into landed Christian denominations.

Another individual that may have had an influence on Dobrolubov's concept of eternal pilgrimage, and especially to central Asia, is the migration of the Bride Community of Claasz Epp, Jr. He deeply studied Jung-Stilling's *Das Heimweh* (Homesickness) and felt that the coming of Jesus Christ was near, that the era had arrived for the tribulation, and that the refuge was in the east, based on the writings of Jung-Stilling. In 1879, he began to preach his apocalyptic views among the local Mennonites of central Russia, which were combined with his study of Jung-Stilling's writings. Epp's vision of the place of refuge was the eastern portion of Turkmenistan or some local region.

In August 1880, about 600 people sold all their possessions and left to travel eastward. The first group arrived at Tashkent, Uzbekistan, after four months of travel. The group pushed on to the city Turkestan, in south-central Kazakhstan. Dissension set in, and the Bride Community divided: some left to Dzhambul, also in south-central Kazakhstan, while another group went to Tashkent.

The balance of Epp's followers migrated to Lausan, along the Amu Darya River, in Turkmenistan, where they remained through 1884. Economic failure forced Epp to move again, now to the final place of refuge, Khiva, in central Uzbekistan, near the Turkmenistan border. After arriving at Khiva, several more abandoned him. As time progressed they also left him, one by one, until he died on January 19, 1913.

The history of Epp's Bride Community is mentioned because Dobrolubov likewise traveled and lived in the same regions and remnants of the community may still have been residing there.

BIOGRAPHY

Dobrolubov was born 1876, in Warsaw, Poland, where his father worked for the Russian government as a civil servant. His family at the time was considered part of the aristocracy and Dobrolubov had access to many privileges in Russian higher society. Otherwise there is no information available regarding his early life. After his father's death in 1892, Dobrolubov moved to St Petersburg with his mother.

He began writing poetry while in school as an adolescent. Once in Russia he dedicated himself to writing and followed the style of western European symbolists and decadence. He attended Petersburg University and studied history and philosophy. With his circle of associates, he smoked hashish and opium, and preached fatalism and suicide. As a result of his moral corruption and bad influence, he was expelled from the university.

During these years Dobrolubov studied John Ruskin, Vladimir Solovyov, Plotinus, Bliase Pascal, Freidrich Schelling, Epicurius, the Bible and especially the prophets, Revelation and the Apostle Paul, the Zend-Avesta, Kabbala, John Bunyan, the apostolic Clement, Francis of Assisi, and even Buddhism. Many of their influences would appear in his mystic compositions and poetry.

In 1895, Dobrolubov published his first collection of poems, *Natura naturas. Natura naturata.* He resided in a narrow circle of symbolists and his poetry was limited to a few readers. For the few that did read them, they were alien and difficult to understand. After his religious conversion, a second book of poetry was compiled and published by his friends in about 1900, and it was simple titled, *Poem Collection*, but its circulation was meager.

In late 1897 or early 1898, Dobrolubov experienced a religious transformation. It was as though overnight he became an entirely new and different person, now with a search for God and mystic experience. First he went to John of Kronshtadt for counsel, and then on a pilgrimage to Troitzki-Sergeev Monastery, and then at the end of 1898 he departed to Solovetski Monastery with the intention of becoming a Russian Orthodox monk. After 7 months at Solovetski, he left, not able to adapt to the regimen, and he began his life-long pilgrimage and nomadic travel throughout Russia while preaching his version of Christian mysticism. One durable conviction of his was that the Orthodox Church with its theology and rites only suppressed the advancement of Christian spirituality, and he rejected the Orthodox religion as an institution. His attitude likewise reached to opposition to the state, and he declared himself a pacifist.

What led Dobrolubov to such an upheaval in his life's purpose was no doubt the realization that his life of depravity and irresponsibility led him to a dead end, and literally. He survived their fatalist philosophy, but 2 others did not. Two of the members of his decadent circle at the university committed suicide, one of whom was named Vasia, and he is recollected in one of Dobrolubov's poems (also in this volume). This devastating event seems to have haunted him the balance of his life.

By 1901 Dobrolubov had acquired some disciples. Two of them were Stepan Nekludov and Petro Orlov. The reason they are remembered in history is because they refused conscription into the military based on their convictions that they acquired as disciples of Dobrolubov. In the city Troitzki, Orenburg province, they were sentenced to 3 years imprisonment. Dobrolubov, as the instigator and propagator of Christian pacifism, was sentenced to 7 months imprisonment, even it would have been considerable longer, but due to the intervention of his mother, who still had some influence in the Imperial government, it was relatively short. It was this period of time that he mentions so often in his *From the Invisible Book*, when speaking of the prison and its walls and the guards and other inmates. Released from prison the authorities accompanied him back to St Petersburg to his family. Dobrolubov only resided there a short while to visit with his mother, and then left to central Russia. It was about this time that he passed through Tule to visit Leo Tolstoy.

In some respects, Dobrolubov paralleled Leo Tolstoy, except his revelation was 20 years later, and he began his nomadic life earlier. They visited together in 1903 and again in 1907 at Yasnaya Polyana, near Tule, and Tolstoy in his diary complements Dobrolubov for his convictions, the 2 of them having many similarities. This also strengthened Tolstoy's convictions.

Once receiving many revelations of the Holy Spirit, and his 7 month imprisonment for being an accessory to his friends' refusal of conscription into the military, he compiled his final set of compositions and published it in 1905, the title being, *From the Invisible Book*. This book however was completely rejected by his former companions and circle of symbolists. For them it was worthless.

Dobrolubov's wanderings up to about 1921 were from Nizhni-Novgorod and south along the Volga River valley, and then to Orenburg, and occasionally back to Petersburg to visit his mother. Residing most of the time in the Samara region of central Russia, and near the Urals, he was able to escape the turmoil of the First World War, and especially as a pacifist, being one step ahead of military recruiters. The region of Samara was a favorable spot for Dobrolubov also since it was very much the center of sectarian denominations, many of whom shared similar convictions. It was no doubt due to the expansion of the Russian civil war and Dobrolubov's repulsion of militarism and violence, that led him and a handful of adherents to leave Samara and migrate to Omsk, Siberia, a region of safety and seclusion from the warring factions of the Red and White armies.

Several passages in Dobrolubov's poems are dedicated to one journey that was west to east across northern Russia, and probably after the time when he left Solovetski Monastery. The journey was across Olonetzki Province from the area of Lake Ladoga (Ladozhskoi Ozero) and east into the plains surrounding Kargopol. Dobrolubov walked the entire course of several hundred miles and depended on the kindness of local villagers for his survival. This occurred during a local famine.

The adherents he gathered called themselves Dobrolubovtzi, and they were few and scattered, separating from Orthodoxy, and denying the validity of the state, and living in isolated communities. Most of them were in Samara Province. Records indicate that most of them migrated to his community from the local Molokans or other sectarian communities, and then later, after the departure of Dobrolubov, they returned.

Once moving to Omsk, Siberia, his efforts at organizing a religious community was essentially at an end. Nonetheless, he would gather a few adherents to meet together, but never anything more than about 6 families, or about 10 to 12 individuals. This was recorded in a letter of N.G. Sutkov to Leo Tolstoy. During these years Dobrolubov worked in excavation or perhaps ditch-digging, (depending on the translation of the Russian word) and in one letter he worked on laying railroads tracks. All of this was heavy manual labor, and the result of never having learned a trade or vocation in early years. His tradition in the region was transmitted verbally with his philosophy of Christian mysticism, communion with God without external appurtenances, including books, and a sincere concern for the welfare of others as the materialization of this divine perspective.

Dobrolubov's activity almost disappears after the Russian Revolution when he moves to Omsk, Siberia, in 1921, since now he was always one step ahead of Soviet police. In 1923-1925, he is near Samara again, and even went to Petrograd to visit his mother and his family; the years of 1925-1927, he is in Bukhara, Uzbekistan, and Dushanbe, Tajikistan, central Asia, far from

Soviet influence and surveillance, and far from society and any social associations.

Sometime about 1929, Dobrolubov migrated to Azerbaijan, probably following the Amr Darya to the Caspian Sea, and then crossing it to Baku, and there worked as a stove-maker. In Azerbaijan, he resided in several villages high in the Nagorno-Karabakh region, also known as the lesser Caucasus, and other villages in isolated areas. He would return to Baku to work. He did some composition while there with a treatise on the benefit of manual labor, and about a dozen poems.

In 1930, he was arrested in Baku for charges that are unknown, but that seem to be vagrancy, and in a letter to his sister Irina he requested money for assistance. He was subsequently released and returned to work.

In May 1937, he left the Caucasus region and visited Leningrad and his sister and family and also visited Moscow and his old poet friends Brusov and Veresayev. Dobrolubov then returned to Azerbaijan in October 1938. In a letter of 1938 to Vladimir Bonch-Bruevich, he explained his desire to return to literature.

In one letter to his sister dated May 28, 1941, he mentions his intent to cease his nomadic life and return to his family. But this could not materialize since by this time World War 2 had started and it was impossible for Dobrolubov to leave Azerbaijan to go anywhere. His final correspondence is a postcard sent to his sister in Leningrad dated December 2, 1942, from the post office in the city Ujar in central Azerbaijan.

Dobrolubov's history now ends, and he probably died shortly after his last letter, sometime in 1943 in Azerbaijan. No information remains about the place of his death either, but some surmise it was in an isolated village in Azerbaijan. World War 2 caused massive suffering and deprivation in all areas of the Soviet Union and Dobrolubov could have died unnoticed and then buried by local residents. He was about 67 years of age.

One of Dobrolubov's final correspondence is a letter to his sister Tatyana and her husband Nikolai Yuzkov, dated August 24, 1940 (translated in this volume). He summaries the life's path of this unorthodox and nonconforming person. The inner voice that accompanied him the duration of his life since his initial turn to God dictated the compositions unheard-of to this time, unknown to the world of art. It coerced him with a handful of pious like-minded seekers of God's truth to serve God in the true manner. This divine passion had become his inherent personality and the voice was its result, as he acknowledges at the conclusion of his life. The consummate summary of his search was the truth as old as the world – God is goodness. He states that he attained the realization of this axiom at the expense of difficult and long wandering, and yet it was something that was likewise expounded simply and clearly by other religious philosophers of his category for millennia before him.

FROM THE INVISIBLE BOOK

ALEKSANDR MIKHAILOVICH DOBROLUBOV

Translated from:

Александр Михайлович Добролюбов
Из Книги НевидИмой
Date: 19-22 июня 2008
Изд: Добролюбов А. Сочинения в 2 тт., том 2.
Berkeley Slavic Specialties, 1983 г.
OCR: Адаменко Виталий

1
REGARDING THE PAST

Regarding the Language without Deceptive or Scholarly Words.
A Warning about those who are called Educated People.
There is only One Genuine Education – after the Image of God.

I am a person raised in what is called an educated society, but God placed me on a different road. I expended several years in isolation and in a religious wilderness, in search and in labor and in silence among the quiet working people. With a child's steps – and this may seem funny to many – I entered the path of belief and conduct, this sincere path of mine.

Living among contemptible people of all sorts, I heard their simple yet profound language and saw that they can explain everything and just as good if not better than the emaciated words of the scholarly.

Among these people I found these very profound comprehensions, these very feelings. I even saw that the genuine treasure is even more hidden than they think, because in truly great people the humility is more profound. Inasmuch as they had no desire to be slave-owners, but remained as slaves, but the importance of there dignity penetrates all and every the most minute of their activities.

Earlier I knew many languages, but there was one I did not know – the truly sincere. When I again met with this society – the one that calls itself educated – their feelings and books were burdensome for me. And truly the collapse from human words goes deep. Where is Isaiah?

Where are the ancient prophets that expressed one all-encompassing thought, cleansing all like lightning from the east and to the west? There these contemporary people divide this one thought into hundreds of thoughts, into thousands of proofs and at the very conclusion ended up at the one and the same. And this is good should it occur this way. There is no end to dividing, but is this called moving forward?

Union, union – this is the word that I discovered among the people. In place of division – the union of all; in place of an emaciated intellect – the all-encompassing spiritual aspiration; in place of the education of parts, in place of the servitude of individual and distinct sciences – belief that is all-creating, yielding its place to the education of the visible world and corporeal labors. But primary is union and belief. And then only will the scholarship of parts be no longer an idol, but only an indispensable activity that is not at the forefront, but is just like every other useful vocation. But that which you call creativity and art and beauty, which you so much deify, this creative spirit even without your agitated worries, fills the entire world and creates only in churches and life, and not on dead walls. As small as the law of Moses is compared to grace, so is presently science as small as the coming science of belief and powerful love.

But the contemporary nations will continue to proceed for a long while on the path of solely irrelevant debate and doubt and division.

2

Do not discredit anybody, even in your home, because a bird of
the sky will transmit your voice.
Proverbs of Solomon

Accept this statement, brethren, as a creed. Forgive me, you the
bad and good, high and low, familiar and unfamiliar, men and
women, children and aged, and all whom my infection affected,
and those whom it did not affect, friends and enemies, those who
remember me and who have forgotten me, those who hate me
and love me and did laugh at me. Forgive me, those who walk
the path of purity, and the corrupt and murderers, those
incarcerated in distant prisons and concentration camps. Forgive
me, every creation and animal and cattle, every free bird, and
the mountains and eternal hills of the world, and the heavens
that calmly shine. All of you forgive me, my sisters, and the
grass upon which I laid on those June days outside the church,
for harming all of you. The steppes respire with heavy
fragrances, while my hand – so accustomed to doing wrong and
for no apparent reason – plucks your silent leaves. Forgive me,
you Angels, as well as all the unsubmissive spirits who have
risen against God, all the daemons. Why was I your helper for
such a long while, helping you to blind others?

All of us are one body. One secret sin, one most secret evil
act, one most secret evil word, adds to the difficulty of all and
loads the yoke held over all the offspring of Adam, and makes it
more difficult for all in the world. And one most secret
benevolent act, one most secret perfect statement, adds to the joy
of all and makes it easier for all to proceed forward.

Lord, forgive me. Distance from me, the sins oblivious to me.
Do not load upon us the sins of our fathers. Accept them all,
theirs and ours. This is why You have instituted repentance and
confession for all, because we are all guilty in the presence of
each other.

3
FROM THE INVISIBLE BOOK

He does not demand for Himself servile worship,
But our life is to see Him;
To repeat His sacred name,
To walk in His presence.

Songs were born in my heart since childhood. When I entered the path of repentance, I held my tongue for several years. Once they opened, I could not forbid them and I sang in winter among the trees on an empty road. Now I realize that this was not a road with signs, but only a trail. And it was one of the straightest and comfortable of trails, and maybe it just might exit to a main highway. Even then you will never exit some distant corner without a trail to follow.

All of these songs were born already fully armed in my heart, they were sealed upon my heart so I would remember them. For several years I lived with one book of life, the life of belief and conduct, and I sang all that I sang, but only for the closest of my brethren and for God. I never thought that I should print them or even write them on paper, and since I never had a disposition toward composition. But now I turn toward books and recognize you as being the wisdom of all the eras, the sacred immaculate books of all times, of all the nations. I saw that a book is one of the most beautiful and immeasurable, miraculous and mysterious instruments among the new nations. It reaches the lowest and trembling of people, and the high and haughty.

4

And the conclusion of the matter is that He is all.
From the book of Jesus the son of Sirach.

I sing of the kingdom that is immutable and solid;
Of the endless King,
The ancient and wise,
Whom no one accepts,
Whose awesome name no one knows,
Whom no one sees,
Whose immaculate voice no one hears, except the Angels,
But they all obey His commands.
His name: One and All,
He is One in Himself and All in all.
But how can He be always and everywhere and nowhere?
He is beyond all time,
His surpasses all love
And every word and every human intellect.
He is the Word of words,
And the intellect of the intellects.
He possesses thought,
He possesses the word,
He possesses the kingdom,
He possesses strength,
He possesses glory,
He possesses activity.
You have disclosed Your most secret name to humanity,
And You accept from their hands
The crown upon Your head.

5

Brethren, He was born in us as though in a den of thieves,
Like the shepherds we did not recognize Him
We haughtily all venerated gilded gods,
As educated magi we long sought for Him in vain.
When He unveiled peace to us we immediately noticed Him,
But we did not immediately all find the straight path...
Do not call anybody Father except God!

Brethren, speak peace to those near and those afar.
I am a trustworthy disciple of the Lord,
I fulfill the command in simplicity,
I do not disdain any work in this difficult land.
I worship truth in the Holy Spirit,
Creating peace and disclosing freedom...
Buy the secret for free, the very precious rock.

Nations, repent and accept forgiveness!
Accept the fire and drink from the cup of passion!
There is no other good word found in the world!
You will not see God without the brethren!
The redeemed are arriving, those delivered of God.
They are established forever on the firm and precious rock.

6

Invisible teacher, Son of the living God,
Lead us into Your invisible world,
From this world of external darkness.
To the pure rivers, to Your living waters.
Your mountains are the destinies of God!
There is Zion, the mountain over the
Mountains and lands and heavens.
And upon us resides the blessing of the invisible heaven,
And beyond the sky is the heaven of heavens where God resides,
Stars in the sky and flowers on the ground.
And the immutable path of the stars is revealed to us
Among the stars and flowers.
Rotating in eternal circles with the same immutable song!
I accept from Your hands all the work You assign me.
In no manner do I reject any great will of the Lord.
Gratitude to God for His inexpressible gift!

7

Death, where is your sting?
Hell, where is your victory?
The strength of death is sin,
And the sting of sin is the law.
    From the writings of Paul of Tarsus

Your cross, Lord, rises high above the stars,
Above the invisible skies,
Above every kingdom of human intellect.
You have installed Your soul in us,
And revealed Your Spirit in the night in the abyss,
But decay and death could not defeat the Author of life,
Because it was unable to restrain Him.
So where is your sting, death?

Abyss, where is your victory?
My lips freely opened against my enemies...
Glory to the One sitting on the throne and the Son of humanity,
Glory to the evening sunset
The light we are unable to enter!

8
A SONG FOR SUNDAY

Rejoice children, Adam has resurrected:
The Father descended upon our land,
And has raised the Son high in heaven,
And the Spirit fills all
The land and the sky,
The visible and invisible.
All is reconciled through His cross
And He pours the new wine upon us.
The Spirit and blood testify:
Adam resurrected, Adam resurrected!

9

Blessed are the timid, for they only will be courageous,
Blessed are those who love, for they will be loved also,
Blessed are the persecuted, for they are pursued straight into
the Kingdom of Heaven,
Blessed are the silent, for they proclaim the secret of God,
Blessed are the persevering, for they carry the lamps of the
Word,
Blessed are those who rebuke, for they are the elder brethren of
the people,
Blessed are the victorious, only to them is opened the
undefeatable path,
Blessed are the continual vigilant, for He is always vigilant over
them,

Blessed are those who rejoice, for this is how God will also rejoice
over you,
Blessed are those who united with brethren and God, for this is a
great mystery,
Blessed are those who pray for one another, for God prays for all
and for them.
His name is – Infinite Prayer and Worldwide Blessing.

10

A person's wisdom will raise his head
And place him in the middle of the congregation,
And he will be astonishing in the presence of the king,
And officials, and their sons.
The king's servants will serve him,
And he will sit as a king in the presence of the King of Kings,
He will sit as a son on the throne of God the Father,
Because he subjected himself to the sole Wise and Immutable.
He loved Him with all his heart like a son.
Glory to the Father and Son for ever and ever!

11

How beautiful are all His actions,
Although we can see them only as sparks!
But who can fathom the thunder of His omnipotence?
Only he who closes his eyes from the corporeal superficiality,
Who speaks truth in his heart.
He hears the unknown language,
Marvelous worlds are opened to him,
Living laws, living Angels will live in his heart.
His heart is expanded.
You have installed the entire world in his heart –
The visible and the invisible.
Glory to the Father and Son for ever and ever!

12
SONG WHEN DEPARTING

Where one or two in God's name,
There all our brethren are gathered,
Those presently alive
And those who have previously lived.

Farewell, my good friend, farewell!
God forgive every person, farewell!
Who can destroy the friendship which is alive in God?
Every time you break bread, remember me.

Remain in truth and I will come to you and be with you,
And we will come to you, all will be with you.
We will spend the evening at one eternal great table,
All of the family together.
All the saints in heaven and on earth greet you!
All greet each other with the holy kiss!

"Will you forget me, my right hand?"

"Will I forget you, right hand,
The decoration of my right hand?
Be forgotten, my right hand!
Your walls are always before my eyes:
I have inscribed them on my right hand."

"Will I forget you, my right hand,
Beautiful city, Jerusalem?
I resided in you as though in Jerusalem,
I saw the entire world in your heart."

13
THE WORDS OF CHRIST BEFORE HE DIED

Then he said, "Do not be afraid that I perish.
And do not fear the power of death.
Rejoice, because I have defeated the world.
I will live.

"Do not be afraid, that I perish,
And do not be afraid of the power of death, my friends!
My death is salvation,
My death is love,
My death is for salvation,
My death is for love.

"I will definitely die,
I have dedicated my life for this cause.
Proceed to liberation,
Have peace in Me,
Proceed to freedom,
Have peace in Me.

"I have defeated the world,
I know triumph.
I assign you the name of brethren,
I give to you one heart.
I live and I will live!
Have the heart of brothers,
Have one name.
I live and I will live."

14

No! We will not die as humans,
And we will not be princes on the earth,
But will be kings unto God,
With God we will be gods.

Then we will have no other knowledge,
Other than – we are God's children.
The visible and all the invisible will disappear.
Blessed is the One Rest!

In the name of the Father of worlds!
Blessed is the One Rest!

15

Farewell, little bird, farewell, grass.
You will not see me for a long while.
I depart to deep dungeons,
I will reside in prayers and fasting.
I depart to deep dungeons,
I will reside in prayers and fasting.

I was the friend of every willing creature,
And desired to love all,
I raised the banner of reconciliation,
I proclaimed freedom to you.
I raised the banner of reconciliation,
I considered myself the brethren of animals.

But you, live and pray
To the sole creator of the ages.
Evangelize peace to one another,
And do not forget about me.

Evangelize peace to one another,
And do not forget about me.

Farewell, little bird, farewell, grass.
You will not see me for a long while.
I depart to deep underground cells,
I will reside in prayers and fasting.
I depart to deep underground cells,
I will reside in prayer and fasting.

16
WHILE IN CONFINEMENT

The patrols are harsh,
You are closer to me than father or mother,
You walls that surround me are high,
I do not see you, yet I rejoice.
You prisons are sorrowful for me,
Yet the sun still lives in you and shines,
It walks in you and shines,
Often the stars will shine,
From the sunset and to late after midnight,
And they disappear with the dawn.
Often the stars will shine...

You are foolish friends of mine,
You are a sage like the sage sitting on the mountain,
Exhausted by sufferings,
Trained to provide nice counsel.
You are the bars on my prison cell,
You are the doors made of oak.
I sit behind your security,
As at the fortresses of kings.
I live like a king and rejoice,
I walk like a king and rejoice.

I summon You, the All-powerful,
I summon You, the All-high,
I summon You, the All-unified!
Your name is freedom.
Bless every incarceration,
Bless also every liberation.

17

Do not be melancholy, do not be depressed, my soul,
Hope, rely, on the Eternal.
You see, Lord, my sorrow,
Whom will You send to comfort me,
Or an Angel or and Archangel,
Or will You descend Yourself, my Sovereign?

And I am Your sheep gone astray,
Only I remain from Your flock.
My enemies lure me away,
They place me on their trails,
They place their traps ahead of me,
And they catch me with their traps.

O, God, the living Deliverer,
Deliver me from these snares,
From these snares placed by malicious forces.
Compel me to love You,
Direct me to Your path,
Upon Your path to truth.

18

You whisper to me, to your brother,
"The flowers bloom more, the hotter the sun."
Let us converse a while, my brethren the flowers.
What are you thinking about?
Are you daydreaming?
Will the dream of the times ahead for earth soon end?
Why does it proceed, flowing like water year after year?
Why do you not aspire to God's light?

Do not run into the distance, nimble rabbits!
Explain this to me, wild beasts,
Wild beasts, rocks of the mountains,
Rocks of the mountains, calm rivers, clean waters.

So do I wander about my prison corridor,
I await an answer from the prison:
Where are my friends?
And I myself have resided in such prisons,
I was a king and slave in all the valleys of our lands,
I forever placed stones into the depths of mountains.

And on that very mountain, like a lion I roared,
And on that very mountain, I provided shade like a leaf,
And on that very mountain, I wept like a human.
Will these dreams of earth ages soon end?
Why do all of you not aspire to freedom?
Or have you abandoned the will to be free?

19

Peace to you, O, mountains!
The silence of the nights is my strength.
I have one prayer, His name is one,
And He is my boulder.

The thick forest, where ascetics wander,
This is my joy.
Where the rabbits hop,
Where the goats of the mountains live,
This is my land.
Dreams and visions are premonitions of the world,
The world that is intangible,
This is my struggle.
Chains, roads, prisons, freedom,
This is my destiny.
The tattered clothes of a wanderer,
Is a valuable diamond,
This is my secret.

20

AN ANCIENT ECCLESIASTICAL SONG

I will not die, but will live,
And I will proclaim the works of the Lord.

I am the image of Your intangible glory
Although I possess the wounds of my mistakes.
Be generous, be generous, Sovereign, to Your creation,
To again adapt to Your likeness,
To be transformed to the ancient goodness.
Again make me a residence of Your paradise.

21

Brother, the walls of the prison will rejoice,
And will flower and live,
And will be covered with thousands of green leaves,
And with clouds of golden flowers.
And the non-manufactured temple will gain the victory,
The temple not made with hands.
And the entire visible world.
And the walls will be moved aside,
And the sky will open,
And the wind of God will blow,
A breeze of subtle coolness...

And all our brethren will arrive and say,
"You have become as one of us.
And we will sit under the tree of life,
And all of God's souls will kiss you with their eternal love,
And the marriage feast will begin,
Whose joy will extent even to this world,
Because love is as strong as death,
And as fierce as the passion of the netherworld.

Place me like a seal upon Your heart,
Undefeated like the life of waves of light,
And stars penetrate through the thickest walls of the prison.

Brother, our prisons stand in God's presence,
And the years and the centuries and all the land,
It is only like an early morning fog,
And then the sun of righteousness will rise forever!

22

I will open my lips in enigmas,
I will speak secrets in allegories,
What I have been commanded from the creation of the world.
Subject yourselves, mighty mountains,
Reply, wild animals,
Listen, nations,
Grow, grow, spring flowers!

The mustard has grown into a tree,
From the smallest seed,
On its branches 2 Angels meet,
They wear translucent clothes,
Holding mighty shields of hyacinth,
Behind their shoulders are wings like rainbows...

The first young Angel stands on his knees,
Removing his silver helmet,
He has a secret name on his forehead,
Whom no one knows,
Except the one who received it.
He has unfastened his shield,
Thrown his spear and sword to the distance.
Upon his shoulders his strength is depicted,
Strong waves agitate his body,
Sparks blaze under his feet.

The second young Angel stands on his knees,
Removing his silver helmet,
All the heavens mysteriously brighten.
Upon his forehead is a secret name,
Which he does not know himself.
The skies are reflected in his blue eyes,
The sun is setting, the stars begin to illuminate.
Doves bathe themselves in the waters at dusk.

He has unlashed his heavy shield,
Thrown his spear and sword to the distance.
His hand plucks a fragrant flower,
Silver and the dew that drips from it is also silver.

The brethren embrace each other in their arms,
They wept, they kissed.
Love is reflected in their bright eyes.
The light blue sky moves,
The bright stars begin to shine,
And every creation under heaven
Every breath under the earth, all say,
"Brother and brother greeted each other.
The groom and bride have married
Into a single immutable union, in God."

23

Glory, glory to the supreme God!
Peace on earth, and peace and more peace!
Praise God, and praise God the more!
Salvation to our God and praise!

And the Angels announced,
"Liberation of the will in the land of slavery!"
Praise God, and even more praise God!
Salvation to God and praise!

24
A SONG FOR THE BRETHREN

Brethren, the Spirit assures,
In all nations and at all eras,
That the era of the Spirit
And immeasurable love will arise,
And this era has arrive, it has arrived.
Have compassion for everyone!

So why should you break a bent reed?
Let it stay green somehow until winter!

Stones of fire will be in paradise,[1]
Miraculous songs they will sing.
People will be silent,
God will rise children unto Abraham from rocks.
They will never be silent in our community song,
Their voice will travel when You release them
From slavery and into the liberated world of Your glory.

The immeasurable kingdom!
The immeasurable kingdom!
The face of the heavens and lands!
The endless ladder of the Spirit!
So shall the wolf pasture with the lamb,
A child will play at the nest of a snake,
And will play with baby snakes.
The snake will feed on dust.
There will be no harm throughout the cliffs of Zion,
So speaks the One,
Whose name is the Lord Almighty.

---

[1] Eze 28:14

Brethren, accept me.
I sought you over all the face of the earth
And found you.
We are glad to see you.
We bless you.
God blesses you.

25
FRIENDS

Do you hear, my friends, my voice in isolation, in the nights, when I in the evenings or at night or daytime stretch toward you and see you, the simple, firm, wise, for the sake of the commands of prudence? I will live, but only for your sake. I want to sit at your all-peaceful feast and my Beloved with us. I will walk, but only if thousands upon thousands will surround my every step, if every movement of mine is directed toward eternity and resides in eternity.

I become melancholy if I notice that I hate my other brethren, both the strong and weak, if my hand is unable to stretch through walls and support the weak.

Today I saw the hall enveloped with light, where all of you sat at His table. The flowering spring was clothed with the stars of your cherries, the golden curls that flowed over all the members of your body.

Is this not a parable? His feast?

Outside the church there is no salvation.

26
SONG FOR FRIENDS

Friends, all of us will stand on the Master's porch with friends and enemies, animals and Angels and flowers and rocks and rivers and children of the heavens. Green leaves cover the patio from the heat, the grapevines pour its wine.

Then he will say, "Friends, I provide to you My kingdom, I decline My crown. I am the slave of all of you, I want to be a slave unto all of you." He holds a towel, He will wash the lowest reaches of our bodies, that closest to the dirt. "I want to wash your feet, and want to always conduct Myself as only your slave. I am your Lord.

"I have provided you corporeal food and life and respiration, and I have provided you the ability of movement. I have constantly walked behind you, brought everything to you, served you. I am your Lord."

In His infinite love, just as a boyfriend with his bride, or like a son with his father, or like a friend among other friends, He will fall to my feet just like the woman who wiped His feet with her hair and covered Him with her holy kisses, so shall He display his infinite love. And this will be awesome for the previous eternal mistakes of His friends. Because He was tempted in all manner just as we are, only He remained immaculate. Often, often did His sorrowful gaze stare into the abyss of sin, and death was almost able to defeat Him. But just one time for the sake of His friends did He descend into the valley of this world.

During these days what is written will be consummated, "And they will be priests and kings unto our God," God, how can I ascend Your throne and attain to Your victorious light? I fear that I will die as a result of my spirit's joy. You are the Spirit that proceeds from the Father that resides in the world, and bringing all people to the Father. Is this why You have loved me with an unrestrained love?

SONG FOR THE WEDDING

A stone, a stone He gifted me. He gazed at me; He wrote my name upon His hand.

No one heard what He named me. He gave me a ring, an iron ring and a gold chain, such you will not find in anybody's home. There is another such ring on His hand, it is distinct from His many other rings.

This day we left the city and walked in His forest and meadow, no one on this day saw me with Him. He said to me in the evening, "Friend, I love all your friends, for the sake of love for you I will tomorrow invite your best friends to my wedding feast. Just tell me their names.

"But can I ever forget you? He is immaculate and nice your friend, and in his face I see your reflection. And after 7 days I will again see you, and then you will stand on these steps, which are higher than all the summits you have yet ascended. The birds I will clothe with other clothes, and new flowers of the field, and will lead them all to My Father.

"Then your star, the human, will be the pupil of My eyes. There is no end to My valleys, there is no end to My days, there is no end to the days of My wedding feast, there is no count of My friends.

"Rejoice! I, I rejoice over you. Not only do you drink from the cup of My true blood, but I accept the fish that you bring to Me on the altar made of earth. Not only do you read My scriptures, but I open your book and I eternally read it: it is so joyful, eternally joyful for My eyes. I bless, I bless you for today. This is for you. I have recorded the names of My best friends, go and love them."

Like a blind person, I replied, "But I cannot really love anyone after Your beauty. I lived today with You, saw Your soul face to face, heard the endless beating of the heart in Your chest."

But He said, "My beauty is My friends. My life exists in the eyes of My friends. Truly more than life do I love them." And the veil fell from my eyes.

28

SONG OF SONGS

Be sanctified, be sanctified, Jesus.
As with the stars of the heavens,
Arise and resurrect us
In imperishable bodies.

He arrived in my valley in the springtime, when birds were mating among the branches of the cherry trees. Upon my hills He stopped His feet, and I followed after Him and sought Him. Wherever he placed his feet, the grass flourished like silver strands.

On Sunday He was walking through the village, and when peace was already settled in my cities, when the sound of the bells greeted those who were still in their beds, who had worked the entire week, when the clear and damp morning began that spring day, when children laughed while on their cots near the stove and biscuits were ready to be baked.

Girls, walking for water at the well, saw Him, how quietly and majestically, yet non-stop, the almost unnoticeable Pilgrim walked through the village along its main road. For a long while they watched, pouring the water from the well into their buckets, and spilling some on the green grass.

The city had been cleaned some time back and Angels stood at the corners of all the main streets.

29

DAUGHTERS OF THE NATION

Sing aloud, O daughter of Zion;
Shout, O Israel!
Rejoice and exult with all your heart,
O daughter of Jerusalem!
The LORD has destroyed the yoke upon you,
He has cast out your enemies.
The Lord your God is in your midst;
You shall see evil no more.
    (Zeph 3:14-15)

You broke your hands in a sorrow unto death.
You gazed directly into my eyes,
You asked me, "Where is the triumph?"
The Lord your God is in your midst;
You shall see evil no more.

All stood in a circle in the same horrible depression
And I gazed straight into your face.
I asked you, "There is a land of triumph?
Their sacred dancing in a circle lasts forever!"
The entire world aspires to it with its chariots.

There is the kingdom of the free, the kingdom of the saints!
From joy to more joy, from life to more life,
They pass through it and you are among them.
From joy to more joy, from life to more life,
They pass through it and you are among them.
I saw all of this with my own eyes.
The Lord your God is in your midst;
You shall see evil no more.

30
THE COMPLAINT OF THE BIRCH TREE NEAR PENTECOST

He was hewing it near to its very root.
He was grinning at the top of it.
Sap was seeping from the cuts like tears
Flowing into its mother, the raw ground.
He gazed at the green grass in joy,
It was painful for the hewn tree to complain.

They brought me as a sacrifice to the invisible God,
Hewing me at the beginning of the bright spring,
They sold me for the great holy day of spring.
All rejoiced at my leaves.
But no one would assist my complaint.
All grinned at me as they passed,
Every person laughing just talked.

31

A vigorous night in Your presence.
Like a slave I committed myself
From evening to morning,
To attend Your church.

The heart of winter passed,
The rains are spent, have stopped.
Exit, my bride,
Show your face, my dove.

Listen! The night is expended,
And the flowers blossom,
You are either my mother or my sister
Or my sole groom!
You are my mother and sister

And my sole groom.

Spring suddenly arrived without notice.
The bushes were covered with leaves,
Behind them a roaring beast,
A roaring lion was lurking.

A smile shines everywhere,
A child plays in the sand.
Child! Do not play, be careful.
Behind the hillock is a roaring lion.
Behind the hillock is a roaring lion.

The face breathes health,
The scythe falls to the knees.
The lips open with a smile.
Behind the smile is a roaring lion,
Just as in the bushes a roaring lion!

This beast devours the entire world,
All the world is aflame from this fire.
This beast is the beauty of lust.
You will accept the sole beauty,
If you believe in the joy of love.

I stood with my feet in vanity,
But I preserved your name.
With one foot in vanity,
But I preserved your name.

Peace unto you, my nightingales,
Peace unto you, all my brethren,
The grains of sand and every blade of grass.
I unite with all of you in love!
I unite with all of you in love!

THE WEDDING IN CANA OF GALILEE

He entered our assembly as a pilgrim, because spring was on every side, because love filled the rivers and boys and children and fathers and girls and all of heaven. He walked through our village and definitely noticed the wedding being held in our home. And He sat on a bench outside near a window, where our young people were dining.

We could not but look at Him, how immaculate was His gaze. And He first said to us, "Friends, why do you sit in a manufactured hut? It is so crowded in there. Let us go into My non-manufactured temple,[2] to all My brethren." And we went to a field and He commanded the heavens and something like dew then covered all the bushes and valleys. This was the bread of Angels, the ancient manna of our fathers. He called the storm — His sister, and commanded her to stop and to bring to us the fragrance of the midday countryside.

Rivers flowed milk and wine. Deer and elk and moose greeted us, and we saw that he asked us to free them. Milk poured upon the grass into a stream. Honey flowed out of the hives as a long river into the virgin forests, where no person had even step foot. We walked to them.

He brought us food from all the flowers. "What is this?" We asked him.

Then He gave us honey from the heart of the cliff and said, "This cliff in the past was inanimate for all, but watch, see the wealth in it, like its mysterious heart! Conclude My union with it, and you will walk in fragrance from morning to evening in all the land, and it will penetrate into your very essence. Instead of tangible water in your jars, now there will flow living fountains of wine. The director of the wedding ceremony accepted Him into our feast.

---

[2] that is, not made with hands.

The entire world was hidden under his poverty-level clothes.
And He revealed His chest and gave us His heart and His body.
He gave us His soul and spirit and His wine.

33
WILL WE MEET YOU AGAIN?

Will we meet with you at the miraculous,
At the miraculous river?
There with incessant praise,
Jesus will we serve.

The river banks are covered with flowers
And the stars of the sky reflect in the river quivering.
There among the currents and among the stars,
Souls are lifted to the heavenly realm.
Yes, we will meet again...

Between us and the river,
An impassible gap.
But at a very expensive cost,
The Lamb opened for us the way.
Yes, we will meet again...

He passed through thorns and with blood
Were His footsteps noted.
Where the blood dropped, flowers with love
And belief grew in those spots.
Yes, we will meet again...

There we will gather the pink roses,
That have flowered where the blood dripped.
Together with branches there will be brought to us
The voice of the Father of endless worlds.

Yes, we will meet with you again
At the miraculous, at the miraculous river.
There with incessant praise,
Jesus will we serve.

34

Forgive me and I bid farewell to you, my dear faithful sister.
It is not fog that has gathered over the steps of our ancestors.
A prophecy had descended among us from the heavens,
A sorrow will pass through the entire wide world.
All the princes of the lands have counseled against Christ,
They are strengthened against the truth, all these gods of the
earth.
The sorrow passed among the flowers and villages,
It is an indifference toward death.
It has poisoned all the quietly flowing rivers with wormwood.

Forgive me and I bid farewell to you, my immaculate bride.
We have married, the two of us, but not according to local
manner.
We exchanged our crowns for martyrdom.
We established the great commandment,
To preserve forever our bodily purity,
To protest forever our immaculate minds.
By such a marriage as though we are married to the Lamb,
And through the worldwide wedding we united with all creation,
With the stars, with Angels, with the seas we are united,
Even with the sinful and the beasts we are united,
Even with demons in compassion we are united.

Just say to me when you bid farewell, something great.
Where will I again see these penetrating eyes?
Where will I again hear your encouraging sermons?
You must appoint, appoint for me a assured place.

It is among the residents of the highest of paradises.
Do not go in the direction of the south,
Do not go along the shining river,
But enter the place that is a quiet wilderness,
That is off the side and toward the east,
There the stream flows into small valleys,
Basins where the people bathe, conversations occur,
There I will sit, a well-natured person.

Upon my forehead the Eternal will inscribe a new name,
There I will converse face to face with the Holy Father.
Over my head resides the fragrant spring.
This is He, the invisible who is all-encompassing.
He will reveal to me your earlier appellation,
And so I will recognize you as a relative.
All of this according to your immaculate person.

35
TIMES OF DOUBT
First Excerpt

These were 2 months of horror. For several years I struggled with idols, one after another I destroyed them. Was I not in slavery? I thought. Is this not idolatry? And finally I was still afraid to worship You, the great Spirit.

I do not want to hide from you, brethren, the days of my sorrow, what occurred to me at that time, to what lands of death I was near. I raised my sword on my beloved altar, on all the treasures in my house, but even then, when I did not yet believe in Him, I was not bold enough to doubt in this lamp of light, in immortality. And this preserved me in the midst of the kingdom of true death, and this caused me to return to Him. Cling to immortality.

All the people approved me as I was on this path and the teaching of doubt. I remembered that I met non-believers and indifferent among the most lowly and simple of people. During these days I became close, and unlike any of the years later, to all contemporary educated people. I extended my hand even to the heirs of Epicures. I walked together with all who were liberated in their life from any knowledge of deity. I saw here an complete new path: in the Buddhist teaching speaking little of God, and the Vedic Kapila, rejecting Him entirely or circumventing comprehension of Him and reducing His power. And how overjoyed I was during those days at the words of Fichte, where he said, "They inspire me with a complete rejection of religious acknowledge of God. He is completely something else."

Lord, forgive me.

I possessed the sentence of death and no longer had any reason to remain alive, and in order for me to no hope only myself, but on God who resurrects the dead.

But then in a clear vision my spirit was again awakened and turned to Him with an unrestrained aspiration, although I was still unable to even call Him by His name.

Some of the following pages were selected from a notebook of earlier years. Although I crucified Him and so wanted to cover myself with a veil to hide from Him – as Moses covered his face with the veil of the Old Testament – but God's Spirit resurrected His crucifixion in me.

36
SECOND EXCERPT
From the Letter

Please endlessly forgive me, all of you who have read my manuscripts of the earlier times when I resided in delusion. I had horribly gone astray. I sowed among you clean seed as well as unclean seed. I supported several worldwide deceptions these previous years, and I supported fallacy in general among you.

It is true I heard said, that honest mistakes will never be damaging enough to suffer death, and they can always be rectified. Lord, forgive me.

God's truth is revealed only when on the path of true purity and humility.

But all of this apostasy was necessary, because only now I realize once and for all, how beautiful and eternal His commandments are, all of them, even the most menial. I saw how horrible it is to depart from them. God permitted me to go astray, so in the end I would negate all of my previous paths to a void.

Forgive me with an endless forgiveness and true empathy.

I would not have believed you! You promised me dangerous places, with underwater canyons, rocks, shoals. You stood in tattered clothes, wrinkles caused furrows in your windblown faces, but I saw fortitude in your hands and gazes.

I believed the ship, my child! I nourished him myself, I knew him, but I did not know the path. It was not constructed of steel like your steamships. It had sails, and on its sides there was not seen any machines or weapons. There was not seen modern inventions. The ship was my child. This alone I know, it will be like a flower, secretly flowering, growing and never to die.

I was vigilant in the fog, in the storm, at night. The ship floated above the waves. In my despair, I did not take food for entire weeks. I tossed all the cargo into the ocean depths. I leaned against the stern, the waves dances into an exhausted face of sleepless nights. My hands steered the ship from the shoals.

When I slept, my eyes did not sleep.

Now I believe you, strong friends, beautiful warriors, searches for peace! I struck many underwater rocks, I read of them in your books, but traveling through the strait, one dangerous and narrow, bypassing the tops of ridges of underwater mountain ranges, I entered the endless ocean. As though riding on a poisonous arrow forward, I flew into the eternal ocean of freedom.

38

My contemporaries! I stand in your presence. It seems you do not need to enter into a struggle with your flesh, with your decaying body, with your evil. You consider all of this nonexistence and a humiliation for a human. You call this love of yourselves, a worry just about yourself. How you pretend! How you manipulated and not even notice!

No! I will not lie as you do. I will not say that every intention of mine is pure. But whose are always pure? You have accustomed yourselves to your ugliness.

No! I am a liar as was the previous traitor! From childhood I was taught to steal. I do not speak and deceive; I steal the truth.

On occasion I remember integrity, but so indifferently. And then I take this whip and banish all of these vagrants, all those who sell and buy from my chest. My anger is sacred.

What do you want to teach me? Do you feel I do not know that it is very easy to acknowledge such hypocrites as benefactors? They are nothing more than endless debaters, verbose self-defenders, manipulators.

Or am I conniving against you? Have I even connived against you, my strength, my freedom? It is because of you that I possess fear.

Who refuses to struggle is a coward. I forbid you to enter into some futile struggle, to act as barbarians in battle. The endless and entire world resides everywhere in every heart. Battle and you will live!

Who assigned me this law of death? I want to live, and so I will live.

You say a law of death exists? I searched within myself for it everywhere and did not find it. Only immortality, and this is will. For a long while my will weakened. For a long while it could not find life without death. But through death it aspired indefatigably. Even in your present mortal life – immortality exists.

The mortal imitates the immortal; it aspires to be eternal and mortal. The thousands of incarnations, these tens of thousands of rebirths, these are the beginning of immortality.

You have forgotten those countries where you resided, because the path is without an end, because all of this is still your childhood that hurries along.

Who forgot, he can remember. At the summit of your staircase I will build a wide platform with a handrail. So did the girl whisper to me, my sister – Life. From there you will gaze around and see the past and even to the very bottom. But it was wounded by your foot, a wound resides on its head, blood flows out of it. But the narrow staircase is without a handrail: how did you climb it?

In all truth you are immortal, because you did not fall. At the top you grabbed the handrail and saw all the past and future.

40

The soldier whispers in a dream before death,
"My heart hungers for victory."

Victory, victory! Arise, my God!
There still remains my love

And who shined on me on this path?
In tears I lie at its feet.

The fragrance of its flowers,
Freedom, freedom, is what I hungered.

O, strength of belief! Strength from the sea
What remains are waves of love.

Although mortal I sit, I again will live,
I will look on the earth.
Breathe for a moment.

O, you laughed at the destitute,
But I am calm. I see strength in my soul.

Comrade, hand! This is the final time
I will look on the ground and at you.

The valiant soldier, loving friend!
I proceeded without fear with your hand.

And I rise, the final time.
I call persistently, my friends.

Friends, seek the final movement.
As the waves of the sea I see you.

He sat next to death, a groan before death,
"Victory, victory, hungers the land."

41
RESPONSE TO PEOPLE AT TIME OF DOUBT

I was a child and lived among children,
And I was impressed how you played.
There was one with whom I played,
Another child whose name was Vasia.
Before his death his niceness shined,
But then he soon died.
The boys and girls surrounding him shouted,
But suddenly and in terror I abandoned their games,
And the tears shook on my cheeks a long while.

Now we have grown and are somewhat wiser,
We read a few books and
Learned to ascertained intellectually.
But, brethren, I have no faith in your strength,
I still see this ancient playing of games,
You children, still jumping and joking.

O, who would be concerned over my first days?
Who whispered something to me in my cradle?
Has a prophet or God guided me my entire life?
Provided me belief and even unbelief on occasion.
Whom do I believe? Whom? I still do not know myself.
To state this using the contemporary language, I am unable.
But still I do not believe you, my contemporaries.

42
My trusting friends, asked me,
"Do not fear, but tell us, good young man,
Why do you wander so many years in the mountains?
Whom are you seeking on the face of the land?
You have been seeking all your life for an intimate friend,
Life will gift you eternal friendship.

"Do not fear, but tell us, good young man.
And we will not be excessively overjoyed for you.
We will be vigilant during dark nights,
And will light our pre-dawn fires,
Penetrating the far distance through the window,
Penetrating the deep darkness of the night.
We will learn all the books of the sages,
We will strengthen ourselves with conversations to midnight."

"I will disclosed to you the truth and correctly.
I sought an immutable language,
And slaves and kings who were honest,
And the rich and poor who were understanding,
Just like lightning descending,
From the east and to the west.
I sought among people, among animals, among the forests.
I heard the sounds of waves, I heard the song of stars.
The quiet rivers answered me:"

"O, heeding, learning, fulfilling!
We will open to you the secret passages.
Your language with the animals; your language with rocks.
But we your brethren have no appellation,
The brethren are all yours: eternally forever and family related.
With the stream and peoples there is another language.
There is only language that is all-encompassing, penetrating,
Like love, like life, like intoxicated with immortality."

"The wild animals answered me.
Lowly people opened themselves to me,
The fountains along the roads whispered to me."
"Seek the language that is all-encompassing
From the east of the heavens and to the west!
So the forests will shake from the voice of your songs,
So the wild beasts will be reconciled due to your song,
So the spring will defeat the severe winter!
So there will be no end to this eternal spring!"

43
RECONCILIATION WITH THE LAND AND BEASTS

Peace and more peace to the mountains,
Peace and more peace to the forests,
To every creation I declare peace.
And the timid rabbits hop.
They love my song, understandable to them.
Every blade of grass burns aflame,
Clear trickles flow out of the fountains,
A pure song echoes beyond the river;
Scattered rocks reflect the fire,
And they sing their ancient song,
The thought that evolved from eternity into the past,
Declared before the beginning of time.
I accept the song of the brethren.

At my feet are mountain goats,
The silent elk lick my hands.
Ah, my animals, you are free!
The path of each is not disclosed.
Go, you, each by its own path,
Only accept the peaceful statements from a human!
Here are bears, for you a conversation in peace:
Do not touch the foal,
Spare the peasants' pet animals.
Ah, you snakes slithering under the homes!
Do not bite us at our village fields,
There is no time for pain for the
Peasants during the hot harvest.

All of you, accept peace, the firm word;
So from now on and not until the end of time,
To celebrate with us the resurrection!
So the winds flow very calmly.
So the alert wolves would remain in their spots,

And not to trample any blade of grass,
And not let the grass to grow this one day,
So on an agreeable day all would agree,
To delve into deep contemplation!

This commandment applies only to this day:
Again the grass to grow firmly,
Peace and more peace to the people;
Peace and more peace to the animals,
They begin work locally and universally.
But this work is life-providing,
Not even a dry leaf will perish,
And no one will even break a twig.

44
PROPHECY

A refutation, a refutation of the nations!
Fire, fire upon all the world!
Nations, accept the prophecy!
Submit to my river!

I lived among you in ecstasy,
My days were passed in ecstasy,
As a child I incurred all sorrows
While an adolescent I often wailed.

My childhood was with austere people and cities.
While in the cradle an arrow pierced my heart.
The large rooms shined like the skies,
The chains extended the shameless nights,
While loudly and alarmingly my friends rejoiced,
They trampled my soul.

Age after age those sorrowful indifferent
Were exchanged in my life:
The evil that was tightly woven with the good.
And there was only the pure, truly benevolent remained,
And there was no threat of evil.

What is impossible will occur, yes, it will occur!
Great days will arise.
And the first will be like the first bird of summer.
The second like the wings of a raven.

Nations and skies and animals and rocks,
Will shine in the potency of strength.
The unknown righteous one will arise from his coffin,
And the blood of his hands is Deity.

But at noon the unexpected horror will be revealed.
The entire kingdom of the saints will gloom,
And the bottomless will arise unto the eternal God,
Over the abyss the high and tranquil and haughtily
King of the abyss in his beauty.
The king of the abyss will be victorious on that day.

On that day the impossible will occur,
The great mystery will arrive.
The temples will collapse and scatter
And the priests will shake.
A prophetess will arise from the lowest generation,
To resolve the wars of all the worlds.

45

I arrived at your home at one time and I do not reject any portion of veracity in your teaching. Let the lowest corporeal step remain, but only at the lowest. It does not just reside in the master of the hut, but also in the hut. Foolish guests arrive and hate the master and only glare at the walls.

But brethren, let us build a palace in place of the previous hut. Why support the steps after their destruction? Since all the useful beams serve an even better purpose.

But all of this will be accomplished only when we will no longer pray on the stage, but we should build using it. And all flesh will be inspired, it will become as a spirit of potency, the worldwide spiritual body will resurrect.

Every grain of sand will be transformed and begin to burn as the sun in His kingdom.

46

I will return to you, the fields and my relatives,
It was to our benefit how you as friends surrounded me,
From the morning and all day, I aspired to you, living rivers,
But harsh people, the blind element,
Carried me away from the heavenly day.

But once I tore from the unpeopled crowd,
And ran to these rivers of mine, the trustworthy, the beloved.

I walked among the forests in simplicity and freedom,
I did not think about the people gazing at me.
It is comfortable for me to be in the company of the lowest people,
The sisters-birds in the forests welcomed me.

Early in the morning once He opened the door to me,
Loudly and secretly He called me – His beloved.
We entered Your mountains and the young animals,
They greeted us at the foot of the cliffs.

I will return to you on the path and days holy to me,
I will return to you sorrowing and living and loving,
All the praises, all our earthly treasures,
And all righteousness I will give on your behalf.

I will cover myself with clothes of gold,
The brilliance of the sister-spring will be returned to me,
I will be clothed forever in while and brilliance,
And will drink the wine of spring with my friends.

This city fought with my purity,
With my faith the best of them fought,
And then they laughed at me,
They incarcerated me in their dark prisons.

So now, listen to this, city. I declare to you:
Your gloom and the beauty of your walls breathe death,
And the prison and your church I will reject and level,
Your own knowledge and belief resides in captivity.

47
IN THE KINGDOM OF LABOR
Song for Work
1901

Bless us, King our Sovereign,
For accomplishing Your work upon Your laborious land,
As for Your beloved Son,
As the young man, Jesus.
Friends, he was a carpenter, on the land for 30 years.
And he defeated the author of sin and father of idleness,
And the King of the heavens was strengthened
As a son of humanity.

So bless us in every lowly work of Yours
Upon the entire face of the land.
Then the work of God is in Your vineyard.
Not in the heavens is found even one
Resting or sitting.
They have no rest days and night,
Your thousands of thousands and
Tens of thousands of tens of thousands.
For You are the Father eternally accomplishing,
And Your Son the redeemer, the slave of all to this day,
And we the laborers are called his brethren,
The elect forever. Amen.

48

So many accomplishments of Yours, my God. I see the kingdom of Your labors.

I see that thousands of Your assigned duties await Your laborers. Work under the supervision of the Master. But in your spare time, work on your own behalf, you have little time to squander.

When He sends you a holiday, utilize it as you would your free days: attend church, pray, breath the pure air of the spring morning. Meditate at night, the best manner to attend to your work, waiting for it to be assigned to you. Ask of elders, friends, and see how they respond to you.

What is primary is to watch how the Master attends to His work. Quietly and intensely He works. He thinks of various matters, thinking of all that surrounds Him.

And the Angel cries, "There is no end, no end to His work, no end to His progress. He does not reject even the most menial of tasks that need to be accomplished, and on occasion will assign major ones, but He asks not to ignore the simple tasks.

49

AT THE LAND
SOME RECOLLECTIONS OF THE LABORING LIFE

Where are you, my beautiful years, when I like an unknown pilgrim lived among the lowly and destitute in all, when I admonished children and reverently entered all the national wisdom and the national work, when winters and springs changed over us like dear, long awaited guests? Where are my friends, you the free, you the beautiful? I entered the river together with you, flowing in the deepest parts of the land.

I gained trust in the steams, I gained trust in education, I gained trust in the wise and strong, you directed the path to me.

Slowly the river flows over the plain, but its path is directly to the sea.

From the hospitable hosts, the clean and strong women, the smart girls, the harsh children, then the adolescents who where not nice even for a moment, but possessed no doubts, from all of you who have not yet ceased to battle against nature, I was torn away. Now I wander near this city as a lost animal, but I see before my eyes only you, your days, your pristine rivers, your worries, your labor.

50
FROM THE CIRCLE OF LABOR OF THE FARMER OF THE STEPPES

The morning's radiance has flooded heaven's entire tent. All have scattered from their reins, recently washing, the horses and cattle stand distant on the plain, almost at the horizon. When you finally harness them, when you finally pasture them, it will already be noon. By the time you bring them to the camp on their heavy legs, all of a sudden all will want to sleep. Some will awaken earlier, cook noodle pasta, awaken their comrades, and the 5 of them will eat with 2 unwashed spoons. And then again until evening they will urged themselves to all the ends of the steppes. With the setting sun they will be unharnessed and not be ignored, even the other sun another time will not awaken those who fall to the breast of the earth-mother.

He just finds a piece of wild honeycomb. Suddenly the mesmerizing fragrance strikes him and he raises his head. No, suddenly all the flowers of the tent are trampled, and by whose hands? He raised to his nose his dirt-encrusted black hands, not washed the entire week. The fingers were saturated with the smell of grass and his black nails – the fragrance. During the summer even the feet of the working people smell with all the flowers from mowing, even with what exudes from under the raw earth.

51

Up to this day, brethren, I did not know what love was to its end, how it can be fulfilled in even the smallest matters.

We arose early on this day, long before sunrise. How joyful it is to work in the clarity of the morning, to catch up to the sister the dawn, to greet the sun when it begins to shine upon the grasses and scythes! My heart becomes excited that autumn, much earlier than all of my friends. I greet every day like a ship arriving from the sea, like the precious cargo of a ship. Then I awakened the others and we arose and rejoiced: better to work in the half-darkness than in the heat, because by noon it is impossible to lay under the canopy and not sweat. The horses push their heads under our canopy and stand over us entire hours. We sleep without blankets.

We sang a sacred song and ended the round-up when they invited us into the camp for breakfast. Along the road we turned slightly to the right and began to quickly undress at the brook. The sister-water invigorated all members, returning cleanliness and transparency to us wearied persons.

Suddenly I saw brother Aleksandr, still wearing just a shirt, walking up to me and giving me a strawberry that was growing nearby. But there were no strawberries that year at all. Five berries laid on my hat. He also gave berries to the others, and the final 2 he kept one for himself and one for the cook.

Tell me, who among is the most benevolent and honorable, and who is most filled with such goodness? For the first time I saw this in all my wanderings. Only because there were many strawberries did he invite his friends. Only there I found full love, where with people and even without people you can stretch your hand to those who have nothing themselves.

52

PAGE FROM THE CONFESSION, FROM THE BOOK OF MY LIFE

Listen to a few words of mine as I describe to you how I traversed desolate places.

It was with fright that I traversed these places. This was at the very north of the Olonetski region.[3] Past the Pudozhski hills, forests and rivers,[4] there was spread in the distance the grain fields of the Kargopol plain.[5] The previous years deceived them. Now they hardly gathered enough potatoes for a month, and many were poor quality. "If good people will not bail us out with provisions," they said, "We will all die of famine before the beginning of winter. Then let them feast at our graves." I walked away very timid. Although I walked without any personal effects, even without an extra change of clothes, it was still difficult for me. No one would acknowledge me a beggar, except the worst of people. But did I have a right to travel through this region, where the mother-earth herself wailed and hurt in labor pains? This was an unendurable cry, the cry of all the land, especially since there shined such a tranquil and clean sky above us all.

This land burned my feet. It was terrifying for me to gaze at the fields, terrifying to enter their villages. In every hut, in every corner stood the premonition – the expectation of famine. This was a terrifying famine. The endless torture, the unheard moans nested around every home as a fog, as a cloud. As soon as a log fire started in a house, the corners were still dark. And this was better than light, since it would have revealed their destitution and dirt and naked walls.

I cannot especially and hardly forget one woman. I met her at the well when the air was still fresh, when the morning light shined over the trees. Every sound echoed far into the depths of the translucent atmosphere. Heavy buckets creaked and rocked

---

[3] North of St Petersburg, in Karelia, including the Kola Peninsula.
[4] The region on the east side of Ladoga Lake (Ladozhski Ozera).
[5] Far north central Russia.

on her delicate and strong shoulders, immovable like a beautiful sculpture that looked like a stork.

You personally invited me to dine in your silent hut. O, daughter of the people! Your husband died from depression at the start of the famine, your hut was large, but old; everywhere damage was beginning. At one time in the past, crowds of people fit and huddled here, their hands and feet were strong.

You said nothing, but will I forget your congeniality? I do not remember your face, only once was I bold enough to look at it, but my eyes were in my heart. You did not complain, but will I ever forget your terrifying destitution? You apologized for the lack of food, you were kind to ask me to spend the night, but I declined. Will I forget your firmness and meekness? I was so overwhelmed by you, that if I was to remain, I would touch your hands and tearfully wail. I would fall at your feet and would not be able to stand again – as a result of your endless immaculacy, for your endless destitution!

Quiet and peaceful children accompanied me to the nearest highway. It was not embarrassing for me to weep along the empty road. The birch trees will not condemn me as would people.

O, people of the north! Destitute, confused, in their forest villages, subsequent to you I traversed many regions, I saw food, and the type you do not even dream about. But it was only you people who greeted a pilgrim from a window, converse with him until evening. It was only you who shared with me your last pot of milk.

In hotels I searched for a useful book in the innkeepers bookshelf or loudly read my New Testament. The New Testament was inseparable from me. Everywhere continued work and evenings, all concentrated on their vocations, greedily manufacturing barrels, shoes, and weaving sandals.

How could I repay them? Did I know so little – in work and in virtue? The hosts who were hunchbacked due to their work hardly even raised their heads to glance at me, but when I spoke, they listened to every word all the more attentively. I knew how deep every word of my fell into them, and it was awesome for me to speak.

I was only able to weep at those emaciated by the frost and the sun of the plains. From the fields through the roads stretched out deep ravines and canyons. In my solitude I could not restrain my tears, and only in this manner could I repay them. And my heart pained without stopping, becoming a parasite within my heart by devouring all of my joy. I fled from that place, but just went from the fire into the oven. I turned at the signpost and took a direct route and through the most forsaken part of Vologda province. I remember only the sick, black faces, the black huts. I remember the dirty children in their bruises and scabs, wearing clothes made of remnants sewn together.

I do not want to remember what I saw. In many homes they refused to offer me food, while others offered me a pinch of salt on a piece of onion, so not to refuse my request. Bread was distributed in thin crackers, and they did not think twice about it.

In the southern regions where bread was plentiful, especially in the rich homes I often received a reprimand, but here not one disdained me with even a facial expression.

53
ALONG THE ROAD

A pilgrim in a yellow thin coat walks along the road. The wide highway is straight as an arrow, dividing a forest into 2 halves. It is still completely dark, but the accustomed feet beat the frozen ground. No one is around at this time, even the shivering comrade would not notice, would not realize, what was occurring in the pilgrim's soul. But in his eyes are the silent tears of prayer for all and everybody, for those perishing, for the stormy steppes, for those floating, for those working, for children and for criminals, for every blade of grass, for the cattle – the sustenance of the contrite peasants – for the fields, for the wild animals, for the free bird, for every speck of dirt, for the sky and land, for the valleys and mountains, for all the rich and destitute of the lands. Peace and blessing he carries to the sisters-birch trees and bridges covered with new snow. He brings peace to the river and strives to know its heart, the manner it lies there under its crystal glass – ice – until spring.

Without interruption the ripe joyful tears fall. They pass deep through the snow covered ground and the snow and ground rejoice over this prayer of love.

Now the sun blazes with its clear fire, the way it only shines in winter. Its silver, blue and white rays shine. Like a thief, sunrise creeps over the entire surface of the land.

The pilgrim wipes his eyes and washes them with snow. Now he must no more cry, as those he may meet will notice.

And his feet motion forward and at night during the day across the hills, where the meadows appear at every descent. Below is an unexpected and unforeseen bridge over a steep river bank. While on the plains the day becomes all the more blue, azure as far as you can see, flat like a tablecloth with roads crossing it like lines. The pilgrim enters a forest, red berry bushes lure the passerby to its frozen clusters, immense pine trees rise into the sky with unrestrained speed: straight, clean, young. Behind them are shaggy huts made of their branches.

Now I arrive at the base where the mountain range begins its ascent. By the time you reach the top, you are drenched with sweat, but at the summit the cold is refreshing, and to run 2 miles to the base will not warm you.

Spring flies before the eyes of the pilgrim, the road is covered with thin ice that cuts into the shoes, now worn, and the bark-shoes only last a few days anyway. If he does not chase the spring, the winter chases him. Then there arrives the easy and clear and warm period, without insects. The first herds of cattle graze in the glades. The forest provides a fragrance that is intoxicating. Every pebble is decorated by the wealth of the grass, there is not one hand that is not occupied with life derived from the ground. The pilgrim completes his road in the mornings along the warm highway. Autumn forces families into harvesting, while the pilgrim is again on the road. The bark-sandals, having walked 30 miles, are worn and no different than walking of bare ground.

But winter to him is closest of all the remaining days. With an opened mouth he breathes in the air, and this air strengthens him for many days. What wind is as translucent as in the winter? When does the dawn radiate more? Like a fire it rises along to the heart of heaven. And it seems that during the winter people are more courteous and hospitable. Winter is a bath for the land: fresh air and an all-cleansing cold.

In the villages of simple souls the pilgrim is greeted from their windows. Even the suspicious factory workers smile at him. And at every road crossing – on the plains, in the forests, on the mountains – everywhere little by little are contrite people, pious sages, scattered. They are absent-minded women, a boy with his dear girlfriends, the peaceful hosts of the steppes, and they all seem to look like my own parents, and are all ready to forgive the elderly. Even bashful children laugh at the various places the pilgrim has traveled.

So he travels his entire life, and becomes ill on the road and finally dies.

54
Precious Piece of Ice
A Parable

Morning rose over the river that quickly froze. Against the crystal surface the clouds and sky and air and silver fields and roads and ice were reflected. Invisible blue rays filled the ocean of the air, lying on the washed branches of the pines, every needle reflected the green, blue, red and silver rays! It seems that the sisters – winter and spring – were now friendly, one measuring for itself the morning, and the other the evening. From noontime it is as though swords penetrate the snow and all the solid packs of ice. Water is on the roads but people go straight for the bridge, begin to pile stuff on the bridge so the flowing stream will not raise it.

Here 2 men carved a canal. They remove 2 ice floes, on the third a precious stone sparkles, a small oval shape. In this stone the entire rainbow is incased, living colors radiate from it.

The workers stared at it, what heat was dissipating from this stone! This is why it was called precious, its beauty even penetrated the harsh hearts of people. One person carefully hit it with a stick to break the ice apart, they removed it with a shovel, but the precious stone was no longer visible. One person went to the edge of the water and shoved his arm into the water up to his shoulder, searching for the stone, but in vain and all he did was wet himself.

But a second person standing nearby said, "No, the deceit is not from the ice flow. Every flower is beautiful until it knows that it is beautiful. God gives beauty to the one who does not worry about clothes or food, to the person who does not stare at himself in the mirror. We insulted the ice flow by breaking it to get this stone. But how will its beauty yield to the most valuable diamond? It is only people who are vain with their pearls and rubies, while the ground is beautified with diamonds and grass and ice and every speck of dirt in the fields."

55
PRAISING THE SIMPLE LIFE

A WORD FROM THE PILGRIM REGARDING
SPIRITUAL AND CORPOREAL POVERTY

"Blessed are the poor of spirit and body."

So said the pilgrim.

It is good, brethren, that you justify yourselves with the attitude that there is no need to worry about your future needs, about your family, about your associates, about food for your body, but tell me brethren, how will a person sustain himself? Is it not by today's labor? If you work today, then God will tomorrow provide your food tomorrow for this work. Every person, do take of yourself. But is it not all arranged, so you would not have to worry?

It is not sin to work; it is sin to worry. Arise early in the morning, pray to the light of the world, and then contemplate on the work for the day: this needs to be done, I need to buy that, I need to go there. But also consider that you do not overstep your bounds!

Today's work is not forbidden you and it is not called a worry. But if you add tomorrow's, then your prayer will not in any manner rise to heaven, and today's work will overburden you.

This is why another rises early in the morning and thinks in this manner, "Alas, I need to hurry and finish what is left over from yesterday, and then I have this something else to do, and I need to see this person, and not to forget to ask him something about the hay and cow and village elder, what he said yesterday." While another rises and thinks this way from early morning, "No, Lord, I will not whine. I will not burden my soul with any trivialities. I will not record on papers or books or even on my mind the work that I need to get done, but with every matter and thought and I will say, 'When you want this done, Lord, place in into my memory yourself.'"

It seems the most trivial of items causes worry, and the large matters will kill a person, and arrogant pride will kill a person. When a person will regularly curb his worries, and especially during the daylight hours, how joyful and precious his life will be! Will he not dedicate the best hours of the day for his farm as well as its flowers?

He is the heart of the world and even His smallest He strengthens if they should just for a moment glance at Him. All of us are satisfied from the Lord, all of us with bread and salt and all we have, and all those who sit at His worldwide infinite table are grateful. And He gives bread and salt to al the world, even dogs eat crumbs from His table, the spiritual and tangible bread, open to all. Only work.

Often I heard from you, the elderly, "How is it possible for a person not to sin and not to worry due to work? And what will evolve from our work? Nothing will materialize the way you think."

But count on your fingers the number of failures. All you do is complain instead of figuring a manner of improving the present. What do you do when you hear God's news? Is this not the reason your effort often just falls through your fingers? And you have lost all the treasures previously stored in your homes.

Brethren, what especially bitters my heart is when I hear such malicious words in a dilapidated hut. God has loved you because He never provides wealth to the people on the straight and narrow path. He instead draws you near to His secret, while you want to destroy all His mercy. You then are just as guilty as the rich, and even more than those who add field to field without end.

Blessing and joy reside in my heart when I see your poor, dark walls, your narrow windows. Do not destroy my peace with your shallow traps. Your gates all wide open. You are just as I am and just as He was – a lowly pilgrim of this land.

Blessed are the poor of spirit and body, because He is all in all. I want to explain this to you, brethren, that guards are unavoidable on our path and the destitution pertains to both the spiritual and corporeal. You say that little pertains to the corporeal, but there is no such thing as little. Something great can be hidden in something small and within a child resides an adult human. Small is also large. If you observe the great in the depths, then even more observe the small on the surface. He also provides us what is on the surface. Who violates even one of these smallest of His commandments, he will be called the smallest in God's kingdom.

Friends, should my heart rejoice if I enter the home of an idolater? And yet I notice that this idolater is peaceful and quiet and lives in poverty, and yet he blesses destiny for all of his life. Should I not rejoice over this instead? Should I stop sorrowing over his idolatry as a result of his attitude? And then I enter another home. Its master is not a pagan, he has no images standing anywhere, but his heart is filled with malice and hate. And even though he may be a Christian, I have no reason to rejoice over him and I should rather not cease in sorrowing over his malice. Then I have the opportunity to spend the night in another village, at the home of a very wealthy man who owns a tavern. And he is so nice, accepts me and provides me with clothes and new shoes for my journey. Should I rejoice over his humility, or rather should I not cease over his wealth, over his deception? And if I was to encounter some malicious beggar, I will always be happy over his poverty and blessing, but in eternal condescension I will carry in my heart a sorrow for his inner idols.

Brethren among such obscure peoples I have encountered some who have lived their entire age in poverty and yet they endlessly thank the All-High. While you, the cunning and evil men of power, should not accuse them. Many of them could have aspired to worshiping the golden calf, just as you do, but this inclination just never resided in their heart, and often the opportunity for wealth passed right by their hands, yet he was willing to share whatever he did possess with everybody. His hands managed to stir some increase as the need arose, and so he remained all his life. In one province I spent the night at the poorest person in the village. From adolescence he hated locks, and in my presence he reprimanded his wife for hiding something in a trunk. How true wealth will grow under such circumstances of love and wisdom, of what true sincerity consists.

Earthly wealth is a tangible idol and I can notice it from a distance, as soon as I approach a house with high gates and iron chains, with a mob of vicious dogs. I tell them, "Peace, my younger brethren. Peace, brethren dogs. You can see that – according to the command – I have no staff in order to irritate you, but only to speak peace and even to dogs." But who was there to calm the owner's hungry dogs?

56
ANOTHER TABLET

The genuine slave is everybody's slave. They say, "Is slavery really a secret freedom?"

Yes, brethren, slavery of love is the secret of freedom. Worldwide sorrow is the heart of worldwide triumph. Compassion, empathy are the secret and root of united joy. Crucifixion and resurrection are both the same. Sorrow over everybody is a triumph and an eternally new resurrection in everyone and a miracle and healing. The one who has never suffered will never experience true celebration. The Lord Himself, the King of Peace, was the slave of all. He helps us all, even in corporeal matters.

What can be higher than this? The person who forgets himself in order to be of service to everyone else, he is king and priest. Otherwise even your spirit will perish.

The only free are those who are slaves unto all. This is what the slaves told me who were on the fiery chariot with the Seraphim. I saw them and in the middle of the streets of the contemporary city. But they quickly relocated to the steppes to the slaves, my eternal friends, to the worldwide brotherhood of slaves.

Brethren, brethren!

In this great contemporary Babylon of knowledge resides luxury. In the middle of this worldwide desert, in the middle of nice and cruel slave-owners, I am your only defender. My brethren are slaves, I am sent here from your worldwide society of landowners.

Labor is victory and life.

57
YOU, GALILEAN, HAVE CONQUERED
SPRING, 1903

Lord, where is Your strength and Your spring?
Where on earth does Your triumph reside?
Return my life to me and in Your heart,
Return to my heart the ancient days,
Return to me all belief and my soul.
Inscribe me upon Your hand,
Inscribe my walls upon Your hand,
My walls are always before Your eyes!
Remember Your triumphant and undefeatable days,
When Your hand led me even in darkness!

Brethren, shout to God in a voice of celebration!
I have encountered Him on my path.
From behind He approached me,
Invisibly He touched me,
It struck me and I fell upon His ground,
He stepped on me and defeated me,
He struggled with me overwhelmingly,
He called me – he who struggled with God
And in the morning twilight He blessed me.

He married me in a mystifying marriage
And no one saw our days of spring,
Only the steppes around us spread out,
One the birds around us chirped,

Only the wings around us fluttered,
Only the songs around us sang –
The visible and invisible.

He married me in a mystifying marriage
My rivers flowed into the sea of seas,
And I saw His name in its sprays,
There is no end to His names:
My Father and my Son, my Beloved,
My elder Brother, my Bride and my Sister,
My Right Hand,
He is my entire life and my soul!

58

Springtime, I walked along the road. And suddenly, after long
doubts, the world surrounding me tore apart like a sheet, I again
saw the heavens and shouted, "My native fields, my native
mountains, what brilliance, what brilliance." It was just like
starlight, like uninterruptible starlight filling the entire sky, like
quiet waves, the kingdom of light was exposed with its
mysterious rays.

How can I explain this in some human language? Since
through this genuine apparition I approached this pristine
world, which is secluded from you by what we call the heavens in
parables.

Just as the heavens surround our entire death, all of our
killings and wild shouts become calm and cleansed!

And the endless song of compassion echoes over my land,
"His name is Endless Compassion."

59

I departed from people to reside in solitude and for a long while laid as though dead on some raw ground that was harvested the previous year. And squirrels in the nearby buckwheat field were perplexed and wondered if I was dead or some kind of new unknown creature. Unseen powers filled the fragrant soil, the expanse became blue like the sea, the surface of the ground flared, and I cried and fought with something within my inner self. All the arrogant figures of the land and sky – the educated of Teman,[6] the contemporary sages and non-believers and the Dawn[7] – they all walked in front of me that day. Finally I raised my head and in the soil's respiration I saw the heavens shine, but exhausted from the intense heat and as though alien to me. But the squirrels along the edges of the nearby field were chattering, playing, running, and oblivious to what I was.

Beginning that day I destroyed forevermore this obsolete perplexity. For a long while I was tormented, how can I understand this, what to say in the land, so not to lie to my brethren, until I see the calm radiance on the unrestrained wings of the wind, until I see Your throne closely and very closely, until I hear Your clear and all-filling rivers. You surrounded me with Your thousands of creations, Your tens of thousands of morning songs. Your throne upon the rock and upon the blade of grass, and on the cliff and upon every object, on the earth and on the sun, on the oak and the birch, and on the animal and on the human and on the Angel and on the son and even on Your enemy. I saw Your throne even on the abyss, and the abyss could not reduce His light.

Rabbits and snakes peacefully played and meandered at Your feet, they peacefully rested, and then valleys and iron mines began to shine with an immutable brilliance and were more beautiful than the precious jewels of the underground.

---

[6] Eze 25:13.
[7] Also, Lucifer.

Your throne was forged from the earth and sky. All the rivers of the ages and eternity flowed alongside, flowers blossomed and were ready to suddenly blossom, the dead rose from the darkness and the redeemed who were cleansed by suffering and Your blood were now immaculate. In one of Your hands I saw the face of an animal who was scared due to the rays emanating from You, but You placed Your playful hand on it and like a child it again listened to Your directives, and Your directed him to a friend in an immortal star, and You cleansed its heart and members with the rays of the stars to become like a star. In Your other hand a man cried in despair, but You showed him the mountains of the land and called them his brethren. And he accepted the command of labor and compassion and began to labor in the middle of Your eternity, since there is no distress with earthly labor in eternity, in the creative victory over the abyss with the work of love. Bending down You ordered him to drink from all the rivers and You returned to him the ancient simple roads.

And Angels shook in Your hands as servants awaiting their termination. You led them through the fire of transformation and Your eternal doors. You revealed to them Your laws, mouth to mouth, and even the grass of the steppes, camels and mice and stars and Angels received their immortal coverings, unattainable by anyone to this time and woven from Your rays. The springtime covered the hills and hovered over the depths of the abyss, cities appeared everywhere.

Who is speaking to me? Who is singing to me? I think, Lord, the sages and all people will just laugh at this.

And I shouted, "To the living, to the living, to the One who lives to the end of time, to the One without a beginning or end, to the invisible, to the Sole one will I bestow my life. I am not You, and You are not me, my spirit is not Yours and Your spirit is nor mine, but I am similar to You, Father."

60
ON THE ROAD FROM NIZHNI-NOVGOROD TO BALAKHNA[8]
1903

The mountains, the hills of the land are my brothers, sisters.
Even the rocks of the road are my trusted friends,
The vault of the sky, the rays, are like my fathers,
The wild animals are my dear brethren,
The calm rivers are betrothed to me, mine for all time.
And peace to you, sisters the stars,
The bright stars, you are the lights of the heavens,
Here are the flowers of the fields in royal crowns,
The sun's rays are joyful messengers,
Peaceful rocks along the roads are silent,
I am in your presence, before all of you
I bend my face right to the ground,
All of you illuminate me,
And the blade of grass, an orphan, is still my relative!

---

[8] About 20 miles north of Nizhni-Novgorod

61

Let us go, friends, the sky is clear, the stars are bright,
Let us go, friends, our thoughts are clear, our eyes are sharp.
With them we will enter into you, the paradise, exalted and
mental.

There we will see the Beginningless and All-Unified face to face!
His weakest ray is still the beauty of all the worlds,
The edges of His garments are higher than every love,
The righteousness of all the saints is only the edges of His
garment.
There we will weep in the presence of our Creator!
Native Father, Mother, Beloved,
This is no end to Your appellations,
The One who created us, do not reject us!
With the suffering, with the compassions, together with us,
You who look upon our sins, resurrect with us,
Resurrect in us!

Otherwise flee, friends, the stone and indifferent life.
Or we will arise and begin all in quiet zeal,
We will gird ourselves with a pristine mind.

Let us go, friends, clear thoughts, straight eyes.
The vigilant nights will place goodness before Him.
What is in the middle of the land's night,
What is in the middle of autumn's death,
My dear and trusted friend arrive,
The beautiful sun has set unexpectedly.

62

WORKS AND DAYS
DIARY OF A PRISONER
1904

Few and evil are the days of the present age.
From the *Book of Ezra*

Be cautious, be cautious, says my Friend to me. Take notice, take notice, right now you were among My regions, you gazed at these empty walls, at this weaver's table, at the quietness of imprisonment, and seldom did you hear any noise from the city square. You looked at all like at unchanging inscriptions for a benevolent journey while in your deception.

You want to know My word? Do not hurry, do not ever hurry, because life is endless, an endless work surrounds your every step as does the springtime surround you, as a large quantity of fountains along the seashores of the region. Remember, every fountain is a son of the heavens, this is your brethren, listen to them all and love, love them all.

If you hurry too much, then you will not be able to read what is proposed to you. Before you only fragments, pages, indecipherable letters, and words sparkle, and the music is not played for you, for the one in a hurry.

Here alongside are 2 regions. In one they only seek a miracle, in the other they desire only to somehow stop or return. But the endless ladder and its path is one – the worldwide transformation, the worldwide feast.

63

We have times that are worth something, we have times that are worth little. Once I sorrowed in my imprisonment and the hurriedly moving unrestrained time became very valuable for me, and it was calm for me and so much was expended that night. In one night a thousand years could be expended. Do not disdain His gift, so He will not regret that He gave it to you!

But again I strengthened myself and returned to the ecumenical church[9] and again stood in the middle of the other-worldly music endlessly filling the church and for the sake of my brethren. God returned to me eternal life. In ecstasy I meditated and contemplated and saw that God was stronger than all the world. He today, this evening, can open the doors of my imprisonment.

So it is testified in the tangible scriptures, "Behold, the slanderer will throw you into prison and you will have sorrow 10 days."[10] He has everything defined to the most minute motion, and my imprisonment is only to last 10 days. He is able to today open my doors.

Will it be well with me then when I bid farewell to this cell, if I sorrowed while in it? And I looked all around and all of it was alive. The bed that kept me when I was under lock within the walls just stared at me with such love, the walls protected me and greeted me, they forgave me for the hours of my sorrow. And I said, but I was not joking, "Peace to you, my sister, the cell." And I blessed it.

And the Spirit of Life united me with all the world and with these stone walls. Because great unfathomable life resides in everything. And the face of the jailer when he looked through the grating in the door was precious to me, as though a long time familiar person who knew me well.

---

[9] Russian Orthodox
[10] Rev 2:10

64

I was sewing, suddenly the door opened and a frightened guard sensed that immediately the chief warden of all the prisons was to enter. And so they entered and stood at the doors – all of my fellow prisoners – the peaceful and carefree. The chief warden of prison administration examined me in detail, "Was the food sufficient? Did I enjoy the work?" And I responded, "These brethren are very many, and very much care about me." They calmly chatted among themselves and then bid farewell and left.

And suddenly in true inspiration I concluded that God again sent me a sign from His book of life. Be so will it be in the future nations, the person who violates the law will be always in a prison, but not a material one. Truly, he will discover himself in a desert, because everybody will fear him. But disregarding the fear the better officials over the world will truly come to him with meekness and ask him, "Do you have enough spiritual bread?"

65

Into my superficial cell entered a superficially tall man and he gave me a superficial book for the holiday. He does this every year for everyone in the entire prison and he senses that it is truly the spirit of love that leads him. But he himself is still in the dark and sorrowful, because he still exists under the guardianship of the Old Testament law. And I then understood. My God is giving me a sign. So will they enter all the prisons of the future nations from evening to morning, but not into a superficial cell and not with superficial books.

But it was not noticeable that it was due to the inmates efforts that the holiday was approaching – the transformation of the world.

So, brethren, be able to read even a visible book.

66

You, my days, are quiet and imperceptibly passing,
You, my days, are my dear brothers, trusted friends,
You rise like a dove over the window of my prison cell every day,
You fulfill God's will.
You, my days, are pristine and calm rivers,
You, my hours, are the rivers flowing from the mountains,
You, my minutes, are the natural fountains,
You are like the stones so beautiful and precious,
So what is the reason that you were gifted to me?
You cause me to radiate like a child!
You, my days, are firm and dependable brethren,
You travel by the unchanging roads,
Every hour, every moment of yours is immutable.
You cause me to radiate like Angels,
Overshadow me, Angels my brethren, with the light of your wings,
Overshadow me, Angel of the evening,
With the inner light, with wings not of this world.

67

Here in imprisonment, it is completely outside of my sight how the days of the land are passing. My window is often closed the entire day, especially if I work. Often I stand at the grating in the door, and when I exit to stroll, only then do I see the sun and light and rays.

"How the sun shines," I involuntarily shouted once, entering the courtyard on an overcast day. The guard stared at me as if I was insane. Thick darkness hung heavily over the city.

But today I needed to shout, "What light!" In place of saying – the sun. Yet the day was still powerfully winter, but the light illuminated as far as I could see.

We approached the bonfire, to warm us in the winter after the harvests are long over, and all the members rejoice at the light as a rest.

Having returned, I sat for a long while at the camp daydreaming and I could not restrain myself from a smile and joy. I thank you, my brother the day, your kisses are all over me. You, the Angel, are one of our brethren and just like any of us, and whoever you might be, I still understood your greeting.

Brethren, let us rejoice for all we have, because all is alive. We are the living, but the omnipotent sun, which is more than us, is it not also alive? And the days and minutes and every place – all is alive.

Walk always in the presence of all our brethren! Purge all your activities and all thoughts and your members, in order that all would rejoice due to your effort, and so not to sorrow or defile anybody.

Walk always among all your brethren!

68
BEGINNING OF A NEW LIFE

I again became a child, the winter passed,
And on the damp roads, springtime breathed,
Until the twilight did my joy motivate me,
And my hand opened my eyes and rubbed them,
And I heard in my bed the summons over the water.

I was a son of the earth-mother and all the sounds of the land
Were so familiar to me, as a child in a cradle,
And again I looked as though at the figures of my relatives
And the native birch trees spoke with me,
And the bare ash and pine trees.

I walked in a great worldwide union,
With every friend I respired as a slave of the same life
You clothed me in an entire festal radiance,
My heart and the sky and the ledge of the cliff.

And again it was fast and easy for my body,
And the city of springtime entered my chest,
Through the window the river rang and sang,
And I arose and prayed after a deep sleep.

The prison walls rose around me,
And winter was thawing all around me that I loved,
But outwardly nothing appeared to change.

Lord, hear me, since I have stopped in front of You!

While it is quiet You reveal even louder the storm, so did I read in one of the scriptures of the land, that You always as the true Father are ready to admonish us.

Why, Lord, do my steps so often collapse? Are You not the one who has led me these entire years? Are You not the one who turned toward me when I was yet an unsubmissive child, and when I had no idea of what was to occur the next day, nor even the worries of the present day, or even retain memories of the past?

I ceased to question You, Lord, and I sinned. Come, the Hidden one, who defeats all desires. Come, even to appear in the most lowly of clothing, as a pilgrim, as a foreigner, come in an imperceptible manner.

From this day I install the final endless foundation, from this day I will ask of You continually, let them, all the people, say that I went out of my mind.

Lord, forgive, forgive me.

I saw Your light so close and I drew away. These people – I said this and again I will now say this – these people infected me. They do not think that You can help even the smallest creature.

But I already entered this room. I was already sitting at dinner with Your disciples, and behold You appeared at the front porch, so pale from prayer and love, but joyful for the sake of Your commandments.

So is not the time for the first wedding? Where is the groom? Where is the bride? Where are his friends? Where are her girlfriends?

And God clearly answered, "Right now, here, because He is alive here. Do not think that He is just a thought or some dead truth evolving from some kind of sages."

He says, "Fulfill even the least of My commandments, otherwise you will not see greatness."

70

And an Angel walked to me and showed me a book and ordered me to write, although I read nothing in it. And then he said to me, "This book is plain, a book of simplicity. Without simplicity I will not show you its secret. Abandon, abandon, your will. Did I not teach you this all these years? Did not your friends sing this with you among the green field before we bid farewell? Do you remember?"

And I said, "Lord, how can I recognize your paths: They demand peace from everybody, while those demand only battle? Did you not lead me earlier? If I erred, I am ready to reject it. But I saw just the weak side, but it was Your true church. I saw it in the morning fog and I rejoiced."

Salvation to God!

71

You said, "I will create, create, build upon My slave a region that has defeated many sorrows of these nations, they will firmly approach the immortal regions and behold, then like the tide approaches the shore, the eras of victory will quietly and from all side will approach.?

Remember, you can be a rock, but you can be as those earlier on the trails that were trampled by children and animals. But you must be only My rock. I will place it, I will hew it, I will decorate it.

I will conclude testament and wedding and union with it.

72

To whom do I speak? How do I convert you, scholars? Where did I seek wisdom and each time it was in vain. And behold, brethren, I announce to you, "He is the one; His name is beauty, secret."

Sages, how can your journey without Him? How can you divide His temple into the sanctuary and vestibule? Why do you speak of Him, if you reject His miracles and His power?

He promised me, friends, beginning with today's evening to direct every matter. He ordered me to place every word before Him.

For a long while I ran through all of these streets with all of these boys of the streets. We were small, but really we were so bad! The years passed, the time arrived I could not depart from Him. I was born in His home, every evening I, the scoundrel, returned under His roof, while in His eyes love flowed and it reprimanded me. As the heavens, as the feasts, as the nights, as friends, someone defeated me, struck me on my ground, took me captive with the light of their eyes.

Then he cried, "Desert, desert." This is what from the beginning He sent me to tell you. For you to abandon your worries about your spiritual and bodily clothes and food!

Obey Him and you will grow like the lily as is promised, as is written. Do not hurry to produce flowers, allow leaves to grow initial for your brethren, even for animals.

The desert, the body's fast and silence – these are the first steps into the temple for you. And did you not know this? Even children know of this. Know that My spirit – even though crucified and even though humiliated – still resides in everybody.

These words of Mine were transmitted throughout all the land and from the beginning of time. Observe from your beginning all the commands of purity and abstention. The fire of love cannot begin to burn on the altar of uncleanliness.

The ancient simply path I return to you. There exists a visible one which if from Me, it is not a mortal faction, but a commandment pertaining to the most obvious and ostensive matter of love, but it is not a commandment of the superficial nations.

This is why they said "And our superficial nets come from Him." But they do not want to fulfill even the smallest of My true directives, directing your to freedom, in order to provide a place for the secret of God, and not to circumcision.

For the secret possesses a very small, very small place, even if I have to leave all the body's movements in My prayer!

74
CHRISTMAS NIGHT, 1903

Only the one who is of the same substance as the Father, who is constantly with the Father, only that person can also fulfill His worldwide will.

For a long while I could only rejoice, Lord, for a long while I rejoiced that night and not even in Your presence. I reflected on my life.

How am I to fathom this? Why did You not initially cleanse me? Why did You not initially push me forward to proceed?

You allowed me to enter our habitual regions of the land filled with death, and I was not to fear them or consider them dangerous.

Earlier I saw insanity and regions of depravity and regions of ridicule. I saw even more dangerous regions. Every road I entered I walked beneath the hand of the proud spirit.

But these warm regions were more dangerous than those regions, the indifferent, for which reason the animal life did not enter me. Almost on one occasion the queen of depravity returned to me, and self-interest, and I almost allowed sorrow to overwhelm me. I did not think I could enter with them into the temple, I forgot, I forgot all that I saw.

How You, the Immaculate, protected me. You, against whose essence it is for Your immaculate eyes to even look upon evil.

Why did You just free me a little? Why did I not see You for such a long while? Why, when I did see You, the veil was still in front of my eyes?

Am I able to remove it myself? Am I able to endure the struggle if I remove it myself? With bitter experience I acknowledged this.

You protected me during the time of my sin. You did not remove from me love toward belief and poverty.

God, otherwise I would not have come to You. Secretly You should have defeated me, I would have then sold You for my friends. My sins I loved.

I will abandon, I will leave all my worries!

I cannot but rejoice. My mind is not upon You right now, Lord, as I am astonished at what has occurred with my life.

For the sake of all who aspire, for the sake of Your friends, do You strengthen me, but it is not for my sake. I see, I see Your life in the eyes of Your friends. It is the pupil of Your eyes. Brethren, I firmly speak to you, I clearly saw. He confirmed me for all time, for ever.

Whose voice said to me, that I should have weep over what occurred yesterday, about the subtlety I long possessed. You forgot my sins. Is there reason now for me to recollect them?

He said, "I declare to you joy instead of fighting. I return to you the victory over the times of the eras. Now you can struggle, and I await help for you."

"The friends of the mornings of my days hate me."

Forgive, forgive, in its entirety. Create my spirit to again be simple. Brethren, I announce to you, "In place of intellect, He gave me wisdom. In place of search, He gave me knowledge.

In great humility, in great secrets, in purity, prudence, in great humbleness, in great mental remorse, in great simplicity – He hides. He is the hidden God.

75
IN THE INNER PART OF THE CITY
THREE HYMNS

The mountain rose high over the land,
Covered by living and fragrant rocks,
Decorated by precious flowers,
Rubies, hyacinths.

And He led His disciples upon His mountain,
The final time to speak with them, but not with parables,
Face to face and lips to lips He converse with them,
Saying to them, "Preach to all creation and to all the world.
All are alive pertaining to My Father, none will die.

Even the rocks will be fiery in His kingdom,
The rocks-brethren will sing marvelous songs in His kingdom."
And he ascended in their few into the invisible residences,
Because the old residence could no long retain Him.

He ascended to the spiritual summits enveloped by clouds,
Into the invisible heavens that encompass everything.
And some, having seen, worshiped the Father,
While others doubted in their cowardly heart.

But I know that You live. O, my friend and brother,
I am unworthy to touch the places Your feet touched,
Even here in the land I see the places Your feet touched,
Even the unbelievers aspire and reach Your rays.
In the desert nights, You approach close to Me,
You converse with me while over my head,
You guide me to Your Father!

O, God, forgive and cleanse, I am sinful.
My visions surround me during the night,
They surround what is born in my heart,
They depart at Your heavenly daybreak.

This is my word to you, malicious illusions!
I speak to you about the living God, friends,
You have passions in your heart, but you are born
Outside my will and in a region alien to me.

O, God. I will penetrate comprehension,
But do not allow me to exit from the walls of the city.
Attentively I will watch closely through the window,
I will recognize from a distance those who approach,
With vain guests my conversation will be short,
With vain guests, although friends, we will be silent.

O, God, I will struggle, but only
If You as a friend will struggle alongside with me,
Attentively I will watch closely through the window,
I will recognize from a distance the unseen strengths,
And a stranger will not enter to feast in the city.

In the land is a place that is fatal and dangerous,
From early morning You lead me through them,
Through a dangerous time, through a dangerous place,
Where the kingdom of the desert resides,
Where jackals wander,
Lead me unharmed until the evening rest.

Peace to you, all the beautiful, quiet, clean,
I will reach you through the walls of the prison,
You are living keys with God and in God.
From this point I give my great promise

To always carry all with myself in all places.

Feast in the springtime in the city behind the walls,
Raise the health-providing cup of love,
I am here in safety with You and with friends,
My visions will not overtake me here.

O, God, forgive and cleanse, I am sinful.
My visions surround me during the night,
They surround what is born in my heart,
They depart at Your heavenly daybreak.

77
A HYMN – ON THE FIRST DAY OF MY IMPRISONMENT

Sing aloud, friends, my birth Father,
The immortal, and all-encompassing,
One of our native songs.

You gifted me a calm joy,
Unattainable to all others,
You shined on me through the window of the prison
The words fade like candles before the sun.

You arrived unnoticed as You always do,
In spiritual, but humble, clothes of love.
Unattainable, all-encompassing, omnipotent!
O, bestow my soul upon Your entire world.

I looked to the right and to the left,
Not knowing that right now my Sole entity will arrive,
With Your word You have hewn apart the entire body,
But You entered into my furthermost corner.

To this prepared hall, to the distant cave,

Forty nights Elijah walked to see You,
And there Jesus prayed on the rocks,
Awaiting news of joy from the Father.

They saw furious storms,
The sand of the desert rose in a whirlwind,
But only in the breath of a fragrant springtime
They recognized You, the King of peace.

With You resides all truth and all endlessness,
As it is foretold in your books, Moses:
God arrived from Sinai, the Holy One from Seir
With tens of thousands, with crowds of the saints.
On the right side the fire of the laws shines,
And all the saints are held in Your hand.

Your firstborn among the sons of humanity is there,
With Him are all 12 disciples,
The unattainable secret is being consummated,
Your wine and soul and blood are in the cup.

Behold, all are approaching the inside of the hall,
The bread is broken, all are eating it,
Behold, the invisible blood pours like streams,
For all the sins of the heavens and the earth!

O, God, accept this body of mine,
Accept, O, God, also my soul,
I am glad to die in the spirit for my brethren,
But You will not permit me to die.
The Unattainable, Immortal, Sole!
You have given me a residence in Your presence forever.

You gave me unattainable joy,
Likewise an unattainable soul,
You shined on me through the window of the prison,
Mundane words fade before Your word.

78

What is beyond the distant cities,
After these vast northern deserts,
Not reaching as far as the forested mountains,
I there saw an ancient and glorious river.
After the thaw the grass grows high,
All decorated by watered plains,
Only liberated pilgrims traverse the region,
Young and unrestrained eagle chicks,
Not subject to the old,
Not dependant on anything and anybody.
There the rays illuminate even the body,
There the nature of death is defeated,
The authority of potency and miracle are declared,
There the earthly resurrection is accomplished,
There even the grasses come alive as sisters,
There even the rocks are filled with spirit and movement,
Along this road walk friends in peace with all,
Friends of God, all rejoicing, all compassionate,
Martyrs for the land of Russia,
All attaining, all forgiving, all justifying,
Illuminated with adolescent joy,
All the seals have been removed from the book,
Abolishing the corporeal sword, the corporeal love.
All wealth, servility and killing – has all been trampled.
Having fulfilled in simplicity His commands,
The small and large, as slaves, as children, they are fulfilled.

Often, Lord, performing some empty endeavor that is superficial, suddenly my entire spirit stops in astonishment, and as though You are guiding all of this, as though You like a playful child are helping me. And here, here, right now, You are directing and this other person in a manner to change my delusion through him, if I have fallen into delusion.

God, from the abyss, from emptiness, from nothing, was I created and summoned to life. This I know myself and have united with myself. Even when I violated Your covenant and broke Your blossoming rod, even then You remained in union with me, my King, my Father, who is at peace will all, my Groom, Friend, Teacher! Truly You, just like my slave, You always carried great humiliation on my behalf, descending into this valley of the shadow of death, am tormented, and almost perishing in the middle of the region of horror. I abandoned myself to You, in whose authority, my King and Friends, is death.

You were the pilgrim traversing the world, and I kicked You aside, did not notice You, as though You were disdained. You reside in the midst of the abyss and death for my sake. At one time all of my members, all the cities subject to me, raised swords against You, while You, yes, You, just prayed for them.

You came to me in the region of my mother to protect me from this mother of mine.

You are my Mother, my elder Sister, my Bride, there is no end to Your appellations.

And Your name is One and Your person is only One.

80

Myself plain and in plain destitute clothes, I come to You, the ancient Plain Person.

I abandon, I abandon my will! In this, in this is my will, Lord! I abandon worry, but not about food, not about tomorrow's day, because I abandoned this long ago. I abandon sorrowful worries about my rectitude, deeds, words, fasts, my prayers. I do not want, I do not want to do anything; it is best for You to command me. For a long while I was perishing due to these worries, but now I will not worry even about my friends. Send to me and tell me, O, Omniscient One, all the actions, all the words and all the feelings residing in Your radiance. You love me with a love that is uncontrollable for me. Your enemies You have long forgiven. Will You now lead me to my friends, Lord?

81

Friend, today You have arrived – You, the calm undefeatable light.

I stood at the doors, and the doors were open and I spoke of You to the firm Israelite in whom there is no guile.[11]

You did not discard Your heavens, but 2 of Your rays quickly, quickly with unrestrained love, quickly with unrestrained love tore into my opened doors. And these rays were filled with music and springtime and rustled as thousands of hanging leaves, and they unrestrained were carried into and illuminated my entire tight cell. They flowed like a bursting fountain in front of my eyes, as a stream of time journeying into the immortal infinity. Then it was motionless.

O, You, the hidden and apparent, motionless and unrestrained, accept today my promises, give to me to always see Your river.

82

I stopped, I stopped my work, I stopped all my thoughts and desires, in order to place before You all my life from this moment, in order to reject the most beautiful rivers of my earth, in order to incline to Your unrestrained river, the kingdom of Light.

Brethren, I heard the sound, I heard just one sound. And I doubted, "Will I not go out of my mind," in an earthly sense, and the sound vanished. But beautiful great Angels all stood still before me with a smile of radiance. This momentary sound evolved from something far more than instruments of many strings, more than any human's heart.

And so I say to You, "Faithful witness, Worldwide trustworthy. You were victorious to the end, to the end You

---

[11] John 1:47

defeated all of my unbelief. You know the type of person I am, what ludicrous doubts reign right now in this land, the type of insulting arrogance in which these nations were born."

While the brethren, the Angels, shined with their smile and light and wings, even in my doubt.

83

This occurred many years ago when I was still residing in overwhelming darkness, but the light shines in darkness. It is stronger than darkness. And in the first truly prophetic illumination, I shouted entirely with unclean lips, "If this is inescapable, then do not escape it. Do not escape the inescapable light."

God said the following to me, "My inescapable laws – do you hear them? My unavoidable paths are predestined for you. Since you cannot escape the unavoidable laws of the visible world, so My time of the unavoidable has come. Speedily, easily fulfill it as an unavoidable command of fate. You cannot but accept it from My hand.

"I have assigned you to observe all, all, and even the smallest and smallest superficial acts and words for every day, hour and moment, if you will follow Me. A simpler truth you will not find. Before the creation of the entire visible world I destined all for My humble ones. Be humble yourself."

Light, the great light!

"As I have humbled myself, humble yourselves also. I approached You imperceptibly without radiance so you would not go blind. I see your great sin, so you would not perish in the regions of your death."

84

I rejoice at the end of this day, because when I proceed slowly, I travel better, faster. To what should I be submissive in order to be happy? Not to intellect, not to superficial intellect, not to secular weapons.

But I began to rejoice today because I acknowledged today that these divisions of the soul into intellect, into love and will are all vain. Some philosophers are arrogant, placing intellect above everything else, other scholars exalt some mystery, others – freedom and conscience. This means that their love is insufficient, their feelings are lacking. But there is one true life, this intellect is incomprehensible, it is the mystery and love and freedom and spirit, the eternally new and unrestrained river that proceeds from the throne of God and the Lamb.

85

A person must not retain contempt, not in intellect or thought or sense or conscience or human rectitude or flesh or knowledge. And even more not to disdain Him in spirit or His summons or His love or His mind or creatures or His unrestrained rivers.

At one time I thought that I could proceed without Him and I fell. Then I began to fear having to work or act. I began to say, "Let Him work on my behalf, because it is frightening for me to rely on my smallest effort." And again I almost fell, and it was my smallest weaknesses that lifted my head.

And then You said to me, "Make your individual person – austere. Isolate yourself from their view and from your sorrow and joy. My son, you are free, you are a warrior! Do you not want to battle? I have birthed in you such a strength that even without Me you are still stronger than all the world, in you will remember Me. Because you are My son, and your freedom consists in this, in this manner you are similar to Me.

Do not reject intellect or knowledge or flesh, but their roads that lead astray.

86

And You disclosed to me that You forgave me of my sins. With a new beginning I proceeded into life, Your life. You defined my days as a crown upon Your head. There, all my friends proceeded and illuminated the entire night in the midst of infinity and expanse and brilliance. And we built Your temple.

Angels with their swords defeated the abyss. They summoned the abyss to life, from nothing, from emptiness they accomplished this and eternally accomplish all.

87

He showed me the weapons and I doubted. Lord, is this not conceit? Is this the manner to defeat the entire world? Is not this region – delightful? Apparently I must not seek anything. I must and want to proceed not for the sake of a reward.

And He showed me His entire region. He led me into His thick forests, and then I saw that thousands of armed soldiers awaited me, waited, some that one more someone would help them. They wanted to enter into the region of eternal spring.

88

FROM RESEARCH

Brethren, I wanted to expound the word about God in more detail and in parts and divisions of questions as do secular philosophers, but God forbid me. He does not command any embellishment or modification or addition or subtraction or exaggeration or presentation or deception.

Only if your hand makes a mistake, then you can correct the error.

We will live in a simple temple and speak and do only what progresses from Him.

True theology, the search for a knowledge of God, is not disclosed due to superficial pride, not with the trend of secular science.

He forbid me, forbid my final personal endeavors.

89
ABOUT THE FINAL FIRE

Behold, I have made the final just as the initial. From that place.

We left with him from the village. We left the elders to deliberate about what we said, we did not seek for any response.

We walked, but where, we did not know.

And he said to me, "Friend, one item I could not decipher in your words. How is the transformation of the world to occur?"

But we were silent a long while and we walked quickly.

We approached unaware to His region, we walked along His fields.

Someone approached us and gave us some invisible wine.

And I said to him, "Brother, why are you asking about this? Do you not see what is presently occurring? Are you drunk? Do you not notice what is so clearly occurring around us as in the past? Is the fog so thick?"

"Yes. You do not notice the clothing of things, your joy now is stronger than your flesh. But just as you have concluded a union even with every blade of grass of the steppes, you penetrate into the heart of things. With every creature you conclude an immutable new covenant. You have gazed closely into every secret of life. So shall occur the transformation of the world. They will not notice clothing. They will not torture themselves over their clothing. And only then will your clothing be beautified."

And again we walked and were silent. And I again began, "Brother, I will explain it to you in parables. I saw one insane person. He greeted me and spoke in shadows, I did not see any bodies or people."

"This is an ancient unadulterated fable, even a child will understand it. No one sees a spiritual body, it is the clothing of the body that people honor. When will the inner person arise in his beauty? Why do his chains rattle. I will also tell you: here is an endless precious staircase. Its lowest step rises from the ground and is almost unnoticeable when compared to the brilliance of the endless large number of shining steps following. So the first step was unnoticed. And then they went insane, began playing with this tree and now moan and seek for rays, while they just blinded their eyes. I will tell you a secret: it will remain, this lowest step, but it will be unnoticeable like a shadow and it will submit to you. And it will also start to shine, and become like the radiance of the dawn. I tell you, the evening shadows blend into one endless shade. In the morning the sun rises. Watch how the long shadows flee on the fields and even into the distance thick forests from the working people as they hurry. Who is drunk with the visible wine, he forgets the sorrows and worries. But what does occur next? He enters another palace. And the allegories are not beautiful, but it is the secular fables that are weak relative to true experience."

Then we heard the sound of a silver trumpet. And I said, "And right now the trumpet is summoning us. Those who rise will vanish from the eyes of the balance."

And a beautiful woman descended over us from the skies and filled for us full bowls of wine and for all creatures and we drank together with the blades of grass. We walked shaking as through drunk.

We do not know where we entered. We entered into the heart of the plain, in a deep plain of the steppes.

"Isn't it time for us to return?" I said to my comrade. "But watch. Beginning this day you are to walk everywhere with all. Do not depart from the ecumenical church. When you are again among them, stand firmly among my brethren. Outside the church there is no salvation. This is the prophetic part – the prophecy of the new covenant, the prophecy of the concluding transformation of the world. As the sun rises higher the shadow decreases, so it will be in the concluding days. Remember that there are regions where the sun at its zenith, at its very pinnacle, then the shadow is removed and all of it moves under your feet. The entire visible world is like the old covenant and mundane ceremony, all of this is just a shadow of the future, but the body is in Christ. Schools of prophecy will be opened in the restored land, there the Omnipotent will teach. Perspicuity will allow all to penetrate their vision through material walls, they will defeat all things. The living portion will not be disdained among them, the freedom of prophecy will fill lips and women and children."

And again we walked and were silent. And again I spoke while we both floated in the ocean of the steppes.

"Isn't the invisible fire stronger than the visible? Didn't our spirit fallen due to sin construct the entire delusional and deceived path of the world? Won't this world of death be consumed by the fire of love? And death will be no longer. Truly, I say to you, I do not lie."

"If they take you by the hands like children and all immediately drive forward to an unfeigned fulfillment of commandments, He will arrive and not be slow about it. So will occur the transformation of the world.

90

ABOUT THE INITIAL RESURRECTIONS
FIRST SEGMENT

You said to the human, "You are created to be free and the breath of My life I have breathed into you, and My spirit is in you, as a bride is tied with your spirit.

Brethren, often He approaches our most confined spaces, destroys all the chains, all our sufferings. Who will apply human words to the music of the sea? Even great rivers are nothing in His presence.

But you are still lowly, human. Do not wait for the ocean, the rivers are sufficient for you. And even God's spirit, which resides in you, is hidden from you, because you tend to crucify Him. Spring blossoms in fields, in forests, in cities, and even in every garden, under every patch of ground and in the skies, but the eyes of he dying do not see it. It is just like a mother that surrounds it, with a fresh calm breeze through the window it comforts his sufferings.

Turn from the beginning to what you have completed. He created you to be free and gave to you a human spirit. It can walk together with the Holy Spirit, but can also walk separately. A creek compared to a river is your spirit compared to He who was crucified and residing in you. But He is only part of the total deity; He is the river of the all-encompassing ocean.

From the beginning the aspiration and illumination in this spirit of yours was completed. From evening to morning see only its secrets. Then God's Spirit will be your friend. When you will cease to crucify Him, then He will resurrect. And only with a river can you float to the capital of the heavens and earth and see the beauty and tranquility of the ocean.

SECOND SEGMENT

There is no end to resurrections in God.

The first resurrection is still on earth, where the human spirit is healed. The invisible light and reliance on His help strengthens the struggle of this person. The struggle of this person signifies much on this step. Divine help here is constant, but it is invisible.

If he spends a cheerful night in the presence of the One who is vigilant and holy, if he defeats food and soul and the world and even his spirit, the secretive will be disclosed. Initially imperceptibly, but soon developing into blinding joy. A person sees Him who was crucified, and He resurrects and even more strengthens the spirit of the human. This is the second resurrection.

But there is a 3rd. There is no end to resurrections. As much as the 2nd resurrection is more blinding compared to the first, to the extent God's spirit that resides in a person, one that is all-joyful and liberating for the person, to this extent is the final resurrection powerful in its effect of His resurrection in a person. There only a part of the All-encompassing resurrected, what was residing in the person. And here the true and secretive approaches near and entirely unites with Him, the One who resides over all the world.

He is over the world and in the world.

Begin with the first step, learn the A-B-C's of conscience. You must be kings over your entire life, over the flesh, even over your intellect and over all the mundane world. Otherwise you will not see the King of kings.

92
ABOUT THE FLESH AND SPIRIT
SEGMENTS FROM ONE RESEARCH

For a long while I was silent and all the sounds quieted, and attentively I gazed about the silence. And I saw how all the drops of blood in all of my veins traveled along their unchangeable circulation. Their music was similar to the music of stars that I heard.

And I saw an endless ladder. All of my members, even the smallest of my parts, each stood on its step. And at the very summit of my ladder I saw how my immortal spirit was exalted over the abyss, a little shy, but constant and rising gradually.

This is the reason you are tied with me, my sister the flesh, and all my members in order to walk after its movement, so to instill spirit into all the world, so the spirit would receive other living clothing and eternally new that will always reflect its movements.

Then I spoke to you, the flesh, "I want to love you, my sister, with a delicate and potent love. I want to embrace you in delight so you would be transformed into immortality.

"I reject all that is devious in you, because I know that you were an Angel. You shined as though wearing clothes of emanating rays from your precious jewels.

"The poor was tossed about by the storm, forgotten, but from this day my eye is upon you, but not for the sake of the present humiliation, not for the sake of your fall due to sins.

"I want your windows to be more precious than rubies, and your walls – than sapphires. I reject your present, material, heavy steps.

"Clothing, bride, my residence, you are land of my betrothal. I do not want to abandon you in your present desolation."

He instilled in me endless compassion towards you.

94

CHANGE OF THE BODY INTO SPIRIT

And the body will become spirit and the entire visible world and even rocks will shine like Seraphim and will celebrate and live and sing.

A wedding, a wedding with the flesh did He announce to me when I abandoned all the corporeal. He said to me, "Now you are in safety. Now you can approach it. Transform the entire visible world by using the sword!"

My sister, a bride that cannot be comforted, who can recognize you? You were swifter than lightning in the midst of His paradise. You never departed from me, wherever I went, you stood at the edge of the abyss and did not fall.

In hand to hand combat you fought together with me against the abyss. From your lips I heard songs similar to the music of the sea. You were vigilant over me during the times of my rest.

You were my land, my land. And He ordered me to cultivate and preserve your mountains, your beauty.

Now they cannot rise, dust has covered all of its members, in dissatisfaction, and it face is dirty. Who will get close to it? Who will raise it? Who will call it their bride?

How unrestrained living in its life has become unchangeably dead in its desolation. The sick insane, it swallows dust from its roads, calling this its kingdom, worrying over dust and its shadow!

All things will become spirit!

95

AMONG THE BOOKS

Lord, bless me to walk calmly, to do good without hurrying, so I do not accomplish it only ostensively, so I do not forget the soul of goodness.

Vain and quick thoughts of contemporary people are now distant from me, because I see Your creek, it flows calmly, quietly.

Lord, You know me. I went among the people, to their teachings, to their books – only for the sake of my brethren – so alien weapons will not defeat my humble brethren.

Lord, bless, so this visible composition will not cause me to stumble, so this visible book would not close Your illumination within my inner person, and the communion of the living covenant with everybody. Although I only understand a small portion, all of these pages, all the sciences, and all the mundane books are like a candle compared to the morning brilliance, compared to Your endless free and invisible book.

Give to me the immaculate word, the immaculate deed, immaculate thoughts, an inexpressible prayer. Preserve me in abstention when I am surrounded with every desirable food. Preserve me in poverty and in corporeal labor, in all Your commandments – the small and great. Give me the testimony, humility, courage.

96
IN THE MIDDLE OF KNOWLEDGE

I will seek Him in the middle of the desert. I will not listen to the endless silence of traitors.

"I have not heard of Him," the desert responded to me.

"He is not here," death and the vitality of youth told me.

He reveals Himself only on the altar of purity and love. Strike the eternal desert silence with the sword of the word.

The entire day I walked among the desert of knowledge, I stared intently into all of its grains of sand. It is just like the terror of the desert, the all-destroying and all-killing emptiness of life. It is the daughter of my mother; she succeeded her mother with coldness.

So much grass spread over these deserts, as far as the forests, along which my feet traversed! When will you see others, lands of amazement?

They have nothing to do in their endless desert. This is why 10 times they have exchanged one place for another of every speck of dust, and because they call themselves scholars.

Brethren, there is no arrogance in my words, but my soul almost died in the midst of your branches of knowledge, among the unimaginable diverse information in them.

I was scared. The abyss – just like your desert – spread widely over my soul. Lions arose from ravines not noticed by eyes, and watched the rising sun from the hills.

I attentively watched you and suddenly looked deep into my soul. It was wounded and my soul complains.

So many children they have destroyed!

Sorrow, brethren, great worldwide sorrow over the desolation of your knowledge, over the fruitless cause. It alone entered my heart and almost killed all those feasting in my palace with my Beloved.

Brethren, this was a sorrow but not pertaining to you, but about the terrible sin of my soul. Why was I glancing at all of these regions that rejected miracle and mercy?

Coarse and cruel superficial people accompanied my soul with artificial music of a large group of diverse musical instruments, and this was called – secular knowledge!

As brethren I was to always accept all of you; in my humbleness I awaited all my enemies.

But God said to me, "This time you will sin in your humbleness. Go and strike all your enemies as did Joshua son of Nun."

97

What is your purpose for living, nations? Who will stop the arrogant minds? Is not endless torment possible? Will they just torment themselves without end?

And the more that a person attains purity or wisdom or knowledge, the more dangerous his steps. He begins to brag and goes blind in his praise. He prefers sin over righteousness. His fears and sins and righteousness are all the same, and his ignorance and wisdom and darkness.

They have woven a deceptive web stretching in different directions, like the deception of the progenitors, the trap of traps.

This trap was called the nature of struggle and the present-day world; this trap is called knowledge. One is not far from the another, indifference and blindness.

Who has looked into the gloom to try to see something? Who learns stupidity? Who gathers all his footsteps as though they are precious to him, except a fool?

Who at any time has seen this terror? Who face to face has stared into the empty eye of this snake?

It has subjected pure children and noble minds to its traps. Its captives just sew to it new rags, if any of its captives is more talented than others.

I cannot, I cannot look upon it! Not due to its danger. Sorrow for myself and for the world has defeated my joy. Why, Lord, have you brought me so close to the regions of the death of the spirit?

Tears, brethren, upon my eyes. You still have not fathomed all of my errors.

They have been adulterous, not only with the flesh, but also with mind and soul and love and spirit.

They have trampled all the child-like flowers.

Then I said, "How will I strike the abyss?"

With unsubmission to it, complete unsubmission. Otherwise how will you summon it to its resurrection?

It can kill you. Arise and yourself strike it. It is insane, let the enemy become its slave. When it humbles itself, you will announce it to your younger brethren.

And do not allow the spirit of doubt to defeat you, as thought it is not His battle.

Who loves, can also fight. Fight against what is in you also.

Who loves, will not harm anybody. He will only wash the dirt from all the faces.

98

DOUBT FOR THE SAKE OF RESEARCHING THE PATHS OF THE SAGES

"Good," I shouted, "Doubt, doubt!" Did the most doubting of the sages approach close to these present-day deserts of mine? There is nothing that is pure emptiness, unnecessary, and the doubt of these educated is one of the paths to Him.

"Good," I shouted. Just as long as I still do not know Him as the consummate ignorant, even as one of those who has no desire for His light. Like Job, like Jacob, I will struggle with Him, whom I will meet in the rays of the twilight as dawn still approaches. Lord, forgive me, give me for one moment to glance into this abyss.

Some type of hope sustains me. I am not afraid to perish in it.

And I raised the weapon of flesh and intellect against all the treasures in my house. I said, "Suppose, and just suppose for a while, that I was only born yesterday, that I have no knowledge of any sort, that my soul is a blank page."

And I looked into the abyss – the beginningless – desolate except for some snakes, an endless blind silence, silence, a place that as though never anywhere had any life or sound, this is what she was like, mother of all the living. And she stretched to me her victorious hands and with her abysmal and beautiful and death-dealing eyes she gazed into my eyes and I almost collapsed over the cliff of my soul. I secured myself only at the moment of terror, only at the moment of my death. Someone with wings touched my person.

And I looked into my soul and I saw this very abyss, thousands of thoughts, entire cities of desire, struggle and light and gloom.

And as soon as I looked into these abysses, having measured them to their very bottoms, I saw over them – Him.

Brethren, truly this is an ancient passage, "Doubt liberates." Only the one who doubts in every soul and in all the world, who loses belief in strength and in spirit and in things, who doubts in beauty and the world, only this person will see Him.

Who has never sorrowed, never feared, never likewise will either rejoice.

O, gloomy people. They call you superstitious, but in your presence all of these great doubters and sages are just children. Only you doubted in all, but you gained comprehension as did the greatest of sages from the beginning of time. How small is this weapon of intellect.

Only the person who has experienced the insufficiency of all sciences and philosophies, having acknowledged the vanity of all branches of knowledge, all wisdoms, the entire flesh and all spirit, only the person doubting in all, only he can believe in Him, whose name is Secret.

"Vanity of vanities," said the king of ancient wisdom. The king of all sages of antiquity, "All is vanity!" Only the One can save.

99
RESPONSE TO CERTAIN TEACHINGS AND BOOKS

I wanted to tell you that often those who occupy themselves with psychological science do not call God – living, but refer to Him as some type of dead, human, fabricated concept.

But there does exist the very true, very perfect, meaning – very living. Only He possesses complete life, because His name is – eternal life. It is easier to have doubts in the present life, than in the life of God. The entire world is dead and it is because of death that life – His life – is confirmed. He is genuinely the living, the immortal glory, the blessed God of truth. And this is not a dead truth of psychological secular scholars. He is the inscrutable mind, the highest intellect that is inscrutable, who accomplishes all that He wants on earth and in the skies.

Of course, many nations understood God very ostensively and superstitiously. As a result contemporary scholars are inclined to suppose that He only resides in the heart and they create Him to conform to the shallow understanding of their mind. These have added, others have subtracted, these have inclined to the right, others incline to the left. Beware of both yeasts – not only the Pharisaic, but also the Saddusaic.

Truly, no one can see the Father, only God's son. But God is not your conscience and not your heart. He is inside your heart, He is the all-peaceful heart and all-peaceful conscience and knows all.

Other than the 3 dimensions of space, there is another secret measure, which I knew, of which Apostle Paul reminded us, "For this reason I kneel before the Father, from whom every family in heaven and on earth derives its name. I pray that out of his glorious riches he may strengthen you with power through his Spirit in your inner being, so that you, being rooted and established in love, may be able to grasp how wide and long and high and deep."[12]

It is not in height, not in width, not in length, not in the solid measures of earth to attain to Him. But in a secret measure, in depth, in the Angelic measure, which is the measure of the son of man, the measure of God's son and adoption, which is more than Angelic. Not above and not below, not to the right, not to the left, not behind, not forward, but in depth. This is the means of measurement now revealed in the land!

The living personal attitude of a person toward God, the vision of God, disregarding all the doubts of the literalists and non-believers, always remains as the chief activity of life. And not a deliberating mood of belief, not ecclesiastical orthodoxy, not even sincere constant purity and piety, can exhaust all that is available. All of these are only portions, only some portions of God's mysteries.

---

[12] Eph 3:14-19

REGARDING MIRACLES: SEGMENTS FROM SOME RESEARCH
FIRST SEGMENT

Not only is there a sun, but also stars. They shine over the visible world, but the true miracle is His unseen.

When the desert travelers sought victory over the visible world, they sought miracles of healing and the resurrection of everything. I will never call this nonsense, so the sages of contemporary education will not also laugh at all of this. And all the more is this possible and obvious, that the visible world needs to be defeated. Because half all of our things that surround us we created ourselves, they are symbols of our spiritual world. We created them and we will exchange them. As our fall due to sin occurred by a person, so by a person is the resurrection of the dead. The invisible fire is more powerful than the visible and the transformation of the entire world will be accomplished by fire.

New strengths will flourish only in the new land. The non-believing science arrived at this dilemma, because it considers the world to be whatever a person represents it. The first miracle, clear to even everyone, is the omnipotent spirit. With whom has this never occurred? Either before your eyes or in dreams, he suddenly sees his close associates and dear ones and converses with them, disregarding the objective walls that separate them. Truly this is no dream. Every occasion, when a person sees some loved one, know that they aspire to you and arrive in your presence and approach your door and speak peace to you. And your response is peace to them likewise, and this will not deprive you of your strength, even though you have been deprived of all the world. Do not subject yourself to the spirit of unbelief. Then they will also see you and your words will also attain to them.

So if the spirit is this potent even toward non-believers, then how much more omnipotent will it be for the one who does see and believe!

A person directs another person and teaches, and a child learns, and he directs the precious soul as he wants, and dominates over younger brethren and often assures them, but to tell anybody lies is beneath him. With a glance the doctor defeats the person capable of being influenced and the one incapable. The beautiful gains the victory with one glance toward love, but all the more does the all-encompassing spirit of belief through his own and in his own.

And if a person is strong and stands on the highest steps, over his friends, he will absolutely transform and defeat the entire lower world. And he will direct the rock and the rock will respond, and the cliff will provide a fountain of living water. And he will forbid death to his sister and she like a mesmerized bride will follow after him. And the abyss will be summoned to attend the wedding with his Beloved. And he will tell the storm, "Silence, sister." And a great calm will arise.

And objects that are not superficial will dominate, but like the ancient desert-dwellers compassion will penetrate the heart of the land and the lions and the desert. And just like the ancient tales of the flying carpet that would move a person wherever he wanted, the impossible will be fulfilled.

ANOTHER SEGMENT

I do not want to speak to non-believers, I want to assured you, the believers, you who are precious to me.

Comprehend, that miracles and the omnipotence of the spirit over the flesh is not against intellect; comprehend, that such belief arises from love.

All that evolves from love is reasonable. What is above intellect, cannot be reasonable.

Who seeks miracles for the sake of pride has died; who wants them not for the sake of love, but for himself, has not observed even His basic secrets and steps – purity and humbleness.

But if He should assign you something to accomplish, how can you deny it? This is what I wanted to tell you.

He want to heal the entire world.

Watch attentively, is it not because of the unbelief that resides in you, as fragments of your previous form, that in you still resides traces of your previous unbelief?

Dead scholars, although they call themselves believers, also have limited His power and also in action do not believe in His omnipotence. You are nothing but children.

O, friends, He will heal, He will heal the entire world! He will curb all insults, defeat death with the sword of transformation!

For a long while I feared His miracles. At one time I even denied what I saw directly in front of me on the road.

I explained this as the omnipotent human spirit, but actually this was hardly a sufficient explanation for me. I even feared being stupid in their eyes.

As a result You departed from me. You raise Yourself a sword against me, fought with me in my depths, until I finally comprehended all Your activities.

THIRD SEGMENT

All of this is only dust, only dust, only weak footprints of those who passed along the roads of the era of my Angel. But now the dust due to Them is sanctified.

How can I reject His strength and where will I place its border, if I see it?

And if you say that an Angel is nothing, that he is just a star in God's presence, I respond, "The sun and stars exist, and if He desires for the stars to die, He can since He created them. There exists and most inner illumination, a revelation of God the Word Himself in the inner prepared hall – if it is prepared and decorated – in a person's mortal flesh. But God can inform a person also through a parable, through every grass, through a person and through Scripture and through a fable and through a vision and through an Angel and through a dream, through a pagan and through a unintelligible donkey.

But even more than through Angels, He works in His humble children, in the humble in spirit and body. Because He is all in all. He commanded us to have corporeal and spiritual humbleness.

Both commands pertain to a person: initially solitude, prayer, the desert, in order to attain the rivers, to draw from it, to converse with Him. But there is also a second: now strengthened, go further to every blade of grass, live and with people and with Angels and with the grasses and with animals. Regarding all and for all!

103
ALONG THE BEL-OZERZK ROAD
1898

And I strolled among the mounds, along the hills, along the roads of the region of many lakes. And below I saw in a row, emaciated horses under the ruthless whips of boys. Behind them slowly and at the same time easily there were wide loaded barges that were motioning along the shining, smooth surface of the lake.[13]

And You said to me, "On that day a person will walk only along the mountains and will not harness any creature and he will watch with his gaze great kindness toward every body. And he will descend even into the valley, where animals are suffering, and beasts and cattle. And he will lead every body to the summit of the mountains."

104

And the person said to me. "How unchangeable is the spiritual beauty of even the momentary flower! Like unrestrained mountains streams, like the dew of a July fog it is gentle and possesses a magnificent beauty. Beauty is His name."

And he said, "We honor every beauty on earth and see His rays in it."

And I heard the song of the prophet Zechariah:

O, how great is His goodness and what beauty He possesses!
Bread livens the children's tongues, and wine the young me.
All beauty is from the Lord,
You who honor beauty, glorify the Lord."

---

[13] horses were pulling a barge along a canal or river

105

God, I sat with the book in the middle of the world, in the middle of deaf walls, in the middle of the hazy light of the land.

The night edged on and suddenly the breath of spring surrounded me, thousands of leaves rustled like strings, like fountains, thousands of brethren stretched to me their hands of support.

I was tranquil like a child, like a person who finally found the road to his native window in the middle of a incomprehensible cold noise of strangers. I knew that even animals, hidden in these forests, sense this together with me.

I see Your road, and You were invisibly behind me, pushing me forward.

The road is narrow; it invisible meanders between the stars, but only one of Your footsteps will fit on it.

Your rays oscillate upon it, Your visit. Only between the distant stars of the heavens, and between the flowers lost in the grasses, does Your road meander, and all so elusive to a person.

You leave the traces of footsteps in many waters and Your paths are incomprehensible.

Salvation to God!

Suddenly I saw Your gaze, it was staring at me through the entire world and while along this road of Yours, uninterrupted and quiet. These were Your attentive and victorious and eternal eyes of Yours.

He watches my heart through all of eternity. He has defined my paths.

So many of Your creatures, Conqueror, but You love even the most insignificant speck of dust, all Your creation. As a person loves and some are often forgotten, but he still has the recollection of the friends of the mornings of his days. Conquer me, O, Conqueror!

As the ocean raises its waves over itself, You exalt me higher than Your lamps.

I saw, brethren, today, this great secret of redemption, of which is spoken among all peoples and not in vain. Profound parables exist in the land, better than any intellect and they are the first of these traditions, the enlightenment of the ancient eras.

I saw how He was similar to a human, so a human could understand Him. And He descended from the heavens onto my land and spilled upon it His blood and at the very moment of death He resurrected and illuminated all, including my flesh. I saw how He entered into this world, into every grain of sand, preaching to animals and plants, even in the netherworld, even in the deserts of fear, in the abyss and to the proud spirit, to His enemies. And He brought a sacrifice – His unrestrained love.

And I shouted, "O, You, whose names have no end, who is called Jehovah, Father, Christ, Mother and Bride and Groom! I saw Your secret.

107

Brethren, He directed my attention to thousands of deceptions in my flesh, even those at enmity one with another – all sons of the same mother. He said to me that the deceptions of the soul are even more dangerous and diverse, and especially to beware of spiritual deceptions – pseudo-prophecy and arrogance of our spirit!

He showed me how a person can defeat the visible world. And opened my eyes to see clearly that alien deceitful powers continually surround all of us. The sons of the abyss enter into your inner city. And you count them as residents of your city and sin by doing this and so strengthen them.

Discern and ascertain the difference between your voice and the alien in order to struggle against them!

This occurred after the clean triumph. I saw as though a city before the holy day, it was saturated with lights, children joyfully watched passers-by, windows of the stores were illuminated, all were relieved of work and were occupied with personal matters. A sound extended from the non-fabricated temple, similar to the sound of many leaves blown by a spring breeze. I saw a star-filled sky, and worlds ascended by an immutable road and traveled along, all these suns and His land, and inaudible music filled the universe.

So were my metal faculties enlightened!

Suddenly in the corner of my chamber I heard somebody's whisper. I glanced in that direction and saw a girl in a plain dress. How she got here, I did not know. My thoughts were immaculate and did not call to anybody. I turned to the window hoping that the vision would vanish, but she was still near to me. She was unsteadily breathing and her shy hand barely touched my elbow. Terror overwhelmed me, because her silhouette was extremely beautiful and her motions were delicate. I closed my eyes, but no matter what direction I turned them, no matter what I thought, she was sitting next to me, and silently and meekly waiting, wanting to present to me her love, to enjoy the evening. Her eyes burned with the sparks of a feast, like the sunshine of a July day they penetrated my eyelashes and eyelids.

And I fought her until total exhaustion.

And suddenly did I clearly and very clearly grasp that this was Your admonishment. You disclosed to me that unseen powers continually surround all of us.

Be cautious of your windows!

And she immediately vanished.

108

This was not a dream, brethren. For a long while I was not aware that an Angel maneuvered right by me.

We were driving the wagon hard. Suddenly some type of swift wings tore across the air and almost right in front of our faces fluttered a quail as though in despair. I clearly saw that all of its feathers were ruffled. Somewhere locally must be its nest. Pyotor and Andrei went and attentively watched, but were afraid at the time so not to step on the chicks. It was impossible to further drive the wagon hard, the hay was barely growing. The hay that year was poor and the master would not have thanked us.

The brethren searched the area, feeling with their hands all the back roads, but nothing was visible anywhere, no nests were noticed, the field was hard like a rock from the July intense heat. Finally we decided to slowly move forward, constantly and attentively watching and listening. The mother bird hid in fear.

Suddenly I heard somebody's footsteps from the camp. Someone was walking along the plain with a noisy and joyful skip, someone tall and strong. I was surprised that this was Andrei's father, but why were his steps so noisy? I wanted to turn around, but the brethren were finishing their search. I increase my stride and caught up to them. No squeak was heard anywhere, not even a wet spot or a burrow.

I turned around. No one was visible on the plain and even as far as the camp in the distant valley.

And then immediately I understood. God sent His Angel in the form of a quail, in order to protect its chicks in the middle of our grass cutting, so we would know that He hears the prayers of all creatures and worries over them.

109
SEGMENTS

And even the corporeal memory of migration is lost among the traditions that zealously swarm over the land.

Who does attain the final step on the staircase of eternity will see in retrospect all the eras of the land. Just with a backward glance he will see all the roads that he began from the initial endeavors of his life.

110

"Intellect, intellect," is what I heard everywhere. But all the emaciated deliberations of these intellectuals were contradictory and did not provide any joy to my soul. I remembered about another Higher Intellect from my life, another cognizance that illuminated me. Your knowledge was disclosed to me.

And I began to research what you call intellect. These clothes were sewn from new material and also from old pieces of cloth, but this is only clothing. I clearly saw that intellect and body are only instruments of the spirit.

All sensations, all rocks, all strengths, all animals and plants, all people's living souls, all that is alive and all the visible, and intellect and conscience, are only instruments of the spirit.

And you said to me, "Watch, do not sin again! You are master over your body, over your word, over your intrinsic strengths, over your mind, over your love."

Many sages have debated over the secret and intellect. And if intellect and secret is what you label as sisters, then one of them is the elder – secret. And a house cannot exist without a foundation and the foundation is intellect, but a house is manufactured from bricks. Secret transcends intellect.

Lord, forgive me, it is just a small righteousness that You have provided me. I researched the mind and meditations of many eras. You are the unfathomable and You do not need proofs. I did not find joys in them, the shy roads are contrary to Your unrestrained illuminations.

You accept my intellect and even body as your weapons, but the only weapon that even exists in the presence of Your secret is my spirit. But You hold me by the right hand, You raise me over the seas like a wave in the midst of Your life, in the midst of Your life You preserve the life of every blade of grass, You give to each their life.

111
THE ANIMAL SOUL AND THE SOUL

The lower soul will definitely perish, but the higher soul He created with His lips, calling it in Scripture – the living soul, or soul or spirit. The vigilant and the living who placed His life on the tree, He gave to me the opportunity to live also on this tree. Do not err, understand yourself, differentiate within yourself the unattainable power and the invisible soul, the mortal and the immortal.

Who adheres to the lower soul will perish.

112
PARTS OF A PERSON

The ancient Russian national song of the *Book of the Dove*[14] says that our bones are derived from the mountains of the land, while our blood from iron ore. And in a person there truly resides parts of all creatures. They have traversed many levels a thousand times and again return.

So it is in the Vedantic scriptures, "I will return to the waters and plants those parts that evolved from them. I will give to the air the soul of the animals, but in you remains some immoral

---

[14] Collection of fables from ancient Russia on the evolution of the earth.

part." One part transcend all the others, as God transcends the world, but God is close to this part because He is close to His image. So did David sing, "God is my portion, God forever."[15]

God is over the world and in the world and fills all.
As the head is one of the body's members, so is He in you.
He is not you, and you are not Him, but He is so close to you, and even though you are nothing.
And movement is due to Him, and every blade of grass reflects His face.
And all the steppes rise to Him without end.

113

Of all that we, humans, know on earth, the invisible heavens closest of all pertain to the human heart, from one side as well as from another side. The only clothes of His bride is the righteousness of the saints, while the heaven of all the heavens is only a temple for Him. We are only the clothing of His bride, but who can fathom her body? And who can explain the Spirit of the groom? And who can grasp the Father?

And the edges of His garment filled the entire temple.

Only the prayers of the humble penetrate all the obstacles and they will not rest until a response is received. And what prayer should not receive an answer? There is no other wisdom except for intellectual humility and there is no other wisdom except for prudence, as it is written, "Truly, You are the hidden God, the Savior, the God of Israel."[16] How will You, the great one, reveal Your greatness? They will not be able to gaze upon You.

The mountains only rise over the valley. What is all the clothing of flowers and kings in His presence?

---

[15] Ps 16:2
[16] Is 45:15

114
FROM A LETTER

I will follow Him to my death. You ask me, Who is He? Truthfully, I do not know His marvelous name, but I know Him. Only He can know His name. Brother, listen to some of these words from one of the seekers of the knowledge of God.

Friend, I am one of those people who believe the words, "Woe unto him who adds to the words of this book of prophesy, and woe to him who deletes something from the words of this book of prophesy."[17] But I do not speak of a literal book, but of the true, invisible Scripture, of the inner Scroll, of the very God the Word, inscribed upon all and resurrected within all. But brother, does this not mean we need to leave the Pharisaic yeast, the reliance on ceremony and circumcision and incense? Does this not mean we need to acknowledge that God's eternal word cannot be confined in any tangible book? Yes, we can we live without a constructed church, and we can find one that is non-constructed. Not only does Pharisaic yeast exist, but also the yeast that adds dead additions and crowded churches to the words of belief. Saddusaic yeast also exists, the yeast of removal, those who circumcise God's power or even completely deny it.

The only person who can walk the path of righteousness is the one who continually turns to God with the prayer, "Lord, do not allow me to add anything to Your directives, do not allow me to delete anything from Your truth."

---

[17] Rev 22:18-19

115

Many acknowledge that a Secret exists – one that is beautiful, indescribable, unattainable by the intellect. And then, how they magnify this secret! They think that they are attaining this secret if they repeat the words[18] of ancient paganism. They descend not only lower than any intellect, lower than even the flesh.

But You are this secret, Lord. And there is no other secret. And You have revealed this to me today.

Lord, I have known this from the distant past – You are omnipresent. But today I saw one abyss and it was so terrifying. I knew that almost all of them crucified You, rejected and did not notice You. But today I came to the cognizance of one great secret. After many crucifixions, often the terror of the abyss materializes – the blood-soaked and tortured calm person. You depart from the unsubmissive city, suddenly, but Your gaze is meek and joyful and filled with such sorrow, such endless compassion.

The clothes of a groom shine upon You, the eternal pilgrim.

Why, Lord, do I often weaken during the struggle, even in small matters, in the smallest of commands.

This is the secret of the struggle, O, brethren! Some struggle on their own, but do not depend on Him. They perform the complete truth, but it is distant from immaculate purity.

Others seek only His help, but themselves in the smallest matters they fold their hands, yield to every sin, they do not even exert the time to struggle with their thoughts.

This is the secret of the struggle, O, brethren! Victory is gained only when your strength is clandestinely united with His help, when your inexhaustible struggle unites with hope upon His potency.

---

[18] i.e. mantras

One motion is like a century, like a thousand springtimes!

I know, I firmly believe, Lord, that visible time is infinitesimal compared to the radiance of the eternal days. You can insert thousands of thousands of years into one motion. You can erase all of the past, all of the hate toward You, all the insults, sufferings, all uncleanliness. And who has not crucified You? And what difference is it if it was yesterday or 5 years ago, in thought or in action.

Do not allow us to be carried away with pseudo-rectitude, because it is deceptive and unreliable.

But protect Your own from every sin. I will triumph, I will rejoice at the worldwide feast of the King.

All of my earlier life is like yesterday. From this moment on You will not abandon me.

Of course sin in our thoughts is great, sin in action is only its shadow. But if you do not release your sin into the external world, then this is the beginning of the struggle, this is a small and it is a large struggle. Because it is difficult to not allow through the doors to the exterior what you have overcome in the inner city. And a small struggle becomes a great one. There is nothing that is small. What is small is also large.

Who is faithful in the small will be also in the large.

Remember this from this day forward and forever.

I have incurred 4 terrors, brethren. I saw all the depths of the abyss.

In the beginning I proceeded under the hand of the proud spirit, and he does exist. He rose against the One who is before the beginning of time and still resides in our world, where earlier the initially created triumph reigned. There we walked the visible world without clothing. All the brethren raced on fiery chariots across the fiery heavens. Diamond sparks flew from under their wheels and Seraphim were born from the sudden sparks. We were like the Creator and we created. This is not a fable, O, brethren. And the songs of some of your poets is just a mundane and pale recollection of this world.

Plants stood like kings and moved in the sun's rays and spoke. The stones were fiery. Chariots met and again departed each in its direction. In unrestrained love some united for all time and this day was labeled the day of the wedding. And the phrase echoed, "Let it be!"

During the initial days after I exited the world, I walked under the hand of the spirit of restoration. Do you understand me, brethren? He did not reject the Creator, but demanded complete freedom and did not accept His paths. He also spoke about love, about endless compassion, but did not recognize anybody higher or more beautiful than himself.[19]

He trusted in me and revealed many secrets to me: other eras will come and his prophets will arise and in our land.

So I drank from the cups of pagans, the cup of ceremony and polytheism and it intoxicated me with pride as wine does the body. as in my past. It taught me asceticism under the name of humility. From the darkness of unbelief I crossed into the darkness of superstition. And then I rejected the wine of the proud spirit and began to fear and debased myself. I definitely

---

[19] Referring to the period of his association with Russian Orthodoxy, beginning about 1890.

believed in the traditions of all the elders, I definitely believed the ceremonies as the immutable clothing of eternal truth. I forgot all my previous education, all of my human scholarship, and just to remember it was heavy for me.

Then a fire destroyed my dead temple.

A new and as though a spiritual wine stood before me, the wine of the visible book and I drank it. I believed the entire literal book, in every letter in it. Then for the first time I saw the Lord, although from behind a veil, because I began to purge my path.[20]

Then the Lord approached me without this veil and I saw him face to face. I forgot about the wine of all the visible books of all the world. But the new wine, the new sorrow stood on my road, the wine of unbelief. I doubted in God, and was He just an idol. I believed only in the human spirit. For a few moments I believed that all was created by human spirit, and all could be enclosed into it.

Alongside stood the wine of the flesh and I smashed the bowl.

I was dying.

Suddenly I saw the Beloved. His eyes radiated with beauty and suffering.

I abandoned all the wines of the earth and skies and ran to Him. And I saw the decayed clothes of the spirit.

"Why are you not starting to sew immortal clothing?"

"Your first clothing, man, is the flesh, the entire visible world. You sewed it yourself. As much malice and killing that is there. The entire world is founded on the river of killing. People kill animals, animals ruin plants and the beautiful grass of the fields."

"God of this age! Listen to me. I am not able to accept this world, no matter how large it is. As long as even one last disdained blade of grass on the steppes is perishing, I cannot forget, and it is my sister.

"While all is still not immortal, I do not accept your world."

---

[20] Dobrolubov leaves Orthodoxy, about 1895.

117

O, how decaying are all your clothes.
The visible world only seems endless, massive.
But it is the filthiest of all your clothes.

Intellect is your other set of clothes.
They do not know that there exists a higher intellect of love.
Their emaciated thoughts are similar to lifeless rocks.

Again I removed the clothing of all my mundane and corporeal sensations. Then I saw the immortal true spirit of mine at the entrance to the temple and at the very top of the eternal ladder stood its Creator, my Lord. His beauty was the strength of stars.[21]

In what language should I speak to you, my contemporary people? All of your education, all of your contemporary cities and customs, all of your towers of contemporary sciences, the entire cold path of your hearts – what a great and awesome desert of horror.
Who of you has seen the flaming chariot of the Seraphim?

Upon the flaming chariot of worldwide love I saw our land – and solely for the sake of love – rising into the heavens and descending into the shadow of death.

And I heard a voice, "The precious stone is hidden from the eyes of all the world."

---

[21] Dobrolubov attains cognizance of the spirit world, about 1903.

118
Final Words

Upon the mountain of silence and life.
Today we will enter, friends, into Canaan, the region of silence.
There does exist a region of silence, where beautiful flowers
grow.
And there are Angels of silence.
Without Angels of God, no deed of any sort can ever be executed.

119

And why not gaze at our beautiful sun?
Or did its rays encounter the enemies?
Or did our Beloved depart from us invisibly?
Or did your clothes, friend, get dirty?
Or did your beauty fade?

Go, my friend, onto the green fields,
Breathe the flowers of the pristine springtime,
Decorate yourself with beautiful gold, white silver,
Drink water from the flowing river of life,
Strengthen yourself with the bread and fruits of paradise,
Gaze into the great mirror,
Into the living and crystal river,
Decorate your youth with humility.

From the east and from the sides
Our Beloved runs as fast as the dawn.
Behold, He enters the green grass,
Leaving behind the royal chariot,
Removing all his military gear.

It is like lightning striking the Beloved,
Before all the world He gives it a holy kiss...
Even stars in the sky unite one with another in marriage,
Even the deaf grass is filled with music.

120

He says, "In My sea, live and be calm.
I will give to you all that is pristine,
And all will be cleansed
As soon as it touches your hands.

Do not hurry where you know not.
Accept from My hands My wine.

Never has my soul rested.
Turbulent like the sea is My midnight sleep.

I will bring Him my hymns,
I will praise Him with music.
He has stretched His strings over my chest.

Thousands, thousands of lives, have I seen!
I glorified my Lord.

Then science and scholarship bend below the feet of He who sits,
Beauty and dignity return to Him.

Then will work and intellect and the body cease
To exalt itself over their King.

121

Passed, passed are your sorrows,
The years of difficult struggle.
Our King, our dear Sovereign,
Consoles you in your city.

News circulates of your battles,
Reaching even to His heavens.
He heard that you fell,
But you could not concede.

This was He during the battle before His death
Who supported your forehead,
At the hour when you raised your trusted sword
In the middle of your enemies.

The final battle, the difficult battle,
My life was terminating,
Suddenly the Beloved comes to me
Yet I did not know that He was with me.

The strengths enter, yes they enter, Your city,
His eternal strengths!
Do not hide the whereabouts of the Beloved,
I seek Him all the night.

Here He comes and He is precious,
His appearance is like a pilgrim:
Imperceptible and contrite,
The springtime hovers over His head.

Animals graze along the shores of the river,
My feet are weary.
If you should fine Him,
Tell Him, my friend, my dear companion,

That I have been struck with the arrow of love.

As a result, God, I fell,
Since You were not passing by.
But now I am with You, the Omnipotent,
So I will continue the battle.

Passed, passed are your sorrows,
The years of difficult struggle.
Our King, our dear Sovereign,
Complains on your behalf in your city.

The strengths enter, yes they enter, Your city,
His eternal powers.
Instruments echo music,
In their hands the swords shine.

122

"Before I would pray for many, for each," said the pilgrim. "I carried them all with me, day and night, at work, when breaking bread. Even in solitude I brought the memory of them all to You. I wanted to live in a manner that every person who would see my eyes would bless God. Whomever I saw but once, I have not forgotten. The entire world is retained in my heart, enemies, those who do not know me and of whom I only heard, all of them were strong and immaculate internal friends of mine. And every day the chains of love strengthened and I felt that it was easier for all for them to proceed. And I knew that I could arrive at your homes, but time did not permit.

"I summoned his blessing upon the field that I walked. I proposed to Him for every visible rock and every blade of grass on the steppes would all shine and be transformed into the land of the living.

"I battled long years with people's idolatries, but I would doubt if this was actually an idol. Can I think that because I

145

placed someone's name before the All-High, that He will automatically shelter him with His grace? Does He not see everybody and all and even without my intervention? I even thought, Is it really necessary for me to ask any of this of God?

And then the fire of love vanished from my heart.

Lord, obviously all of this evolved inevitably from my doubt, and through which You have led me. You even led my soul through its crucifixion.

I turned to prayer, but prayed for all. I feared to perform idolatry with those whose names I asked for Your blessing.

And then this night arrived, the holy night of Your revelation. For a long while I prayed for many, those whom I saw, but after those days ended, I did not bring all their recollection as my offering to the bottom of Your feet. Imperceptibly You entered into me, a person nothing more than a long abandoned and sorrowful besieged city. And I saw my close associates, how slowing and sorrowfully they walked. And motionless did I lie until midnight at Your feet and again beseeched You on their behalf, on behalf of my friends' friends, on behalf of the living and the dead, my enemies and Yours. And again I remembered the names of them all and the entire world entered my heart.

Brethren, friends, world, peace be unto you.

And again you arrived and surrounded me and during the night and during the day and in dreams and at work. You invite me to His marriage feast.

123
A PSALM FOR SUNDAY

The ancient holy day of Trumpets over the land is announced!
Trumpet in His presence as a memorial and recollection!

His Son resurrected early this morning on the first day of the
week,
And appeared in love to His sister Mary Magdalene.

Friends, she stood at the area of the graves,
She prayed and gazed in the area of the graves.

She thought that this was the gardener of the gardens of
paradise,
She said to him, "Tell me, in what type of houses does my master
reside?

You know all of these gardens, gardener.
Is he retained as all the ancients are, in places of gloom and
terror?

Or rather did a fiery chariot accompanied by Seraphim greet
Him?
Now it is morning, the spring winds breeze across the land."

And he tells her, "Mary, my sister."
"Dear teacher. Brother," she cried and fell at His feet.

He says to her, "Rejoice and do not die, beloved!
But you still must not yet grab me.

When I ascend to the pinnacle of the mountains,
Then endless love will unite Me with you forever.

The higher that you ascend, My friends,
The closer that our paths will merge.

It is not tight on His roads,
There the secret of the endless wedding will be consummated."

And she said nothing to anybody, because of her fear.
Then she revealed this to those who were with Him, weeping and
wailing.

On that day in the evening, two pilgrims were walking to
Emmaus,
And in another form He approached them and walked with
them.

Because His light was fill of unendurable glory,
And even to this day, our world cannot contain all of it.

As much as they were able to absorb, so much did He disclose to
them,
But their eyes were restrained by the veil of the law.

And they said to Him, "We have doubts,
Some of our women saw Him.

We wanted to see Him, but still have not seen Him,
Why was this need for His verdict of guilty?"

And the traveler said, "O, slow of hearts!
Is it not by suffering, it is not by death, the path to the kingdom
of glory?"

And they approached near the village which was their intent,
And the traveler wanted to go further along the road to the
desert.

But they began to restrain the traveler,
"Dew is already on the ground, the tops of the mountains are
becoming dark.

The day has already declined to evening and beginning its rest.
Remain with us the night, just as one of us."

And he entered the room and remained with them,
And at dinner first took the bread and broke it for all of them

And their eyes were opened with the light of love,
And they recognized Him, but He was no longer there.

Immediately He vanished in their presence,
And they said to one another all the night to the morning along
the road,

"Did not our hearts burn in us,
When he explained to us the soul of the Scriptures?"

That day Peter also saw him,
But no one ever heard of the manner that he saw Him.

How can the speed and brilliance of light be expressed in a
human language?
Even the Angelic languages are nothing to Him.

His hands shined like rays emanating from expensive brilliant
rubies,
These were the traces of His corporeal wounds.

And all His faithful gathered upon His mountain,
And He ascended in their view to the invisible residences.

But some doubted and did not see Him,
And even the fiery Seraphim long shined with Him during the
ascent.

God permitted Him to reveal Himself, but not to all people,
The fore-ordained witnesses ate and drank with Him after His resurrection.

And they began their imperceptible work,
The worldwide initiation of fishing was announced throughout all the land.

As they were fishing themselves He approached them,
But they did not recognize that this was Jesus.

The Angelic altar burned on the ground,
This fire did not affect human hands.

Upon the altar was placed a mysterious dinner,
And bread and salt and wine and flesh and blood and fish.

And none of them was bold enough to ask Him ,"Who are you?"
And He was immediately recognized when they broke bread.

Declare, friends, the ancient holy day of the Trumpets of the land,
Trumpet in the presence of Jehovah in recollection!

His son resurrected early on the first day of the week,
And appeared in love to His sister, Mary Magdalene.

124

One of the sons of Jehovah was working on one mountain with the sons of Israel.

A Jewish scholar from a neighboring populated city was traveling someplace for business dealing with his vocation, but he turned from the road, left his horse at the foot of the mountain and started to climb it.

The day was very hot, the time to cut the king's fields, the time to cut beans for cattle feed. The scholar was unaccustomed to the heat due to his indoor type of work, he was a tailor.

When he reached the summit, the people had already dined and rested. They held their blades in their hands and inspected the cuttings and were ready to leave their camp for the day. The scholar approached the wanderer, one of the sons of Jehovah.

He proposed several questions to him, hoping that he did not squander so much time turning off the road and walking up the mountain. But the guest just dropped his head and was silent. But the scholar persistently demanded answers and added even more questions about God's kingdom. His tongue speedily moved and he easily spoke of the law as he would of his vocation.

"Brother, right now there is no word in my heart. I cannot speak," answered the interrogated. "If God does not speak, they how can I speak?"

The scholar became irritated. He was convinced that he purchased the Holy Spirit with his zeal and the guest was obliged to answer him, but now was wasting his time. To the scholar the guest just did not want to understanding anything, and so he again asked him.

A young man was standing nearby and became filled with Holy Spirit and spoke and all saw how his word was like light, as a pristine spring breeze. He said, "Who indiscriminately demands someone to talk to him, even it be about the law, who should disdain silence, who does not know how to keep silent himself and will not allow silence for others, himself has no belief in God. Such a person does not believe that God is omnipresent and omniscient. He does not believe that God resides in silence either. For him, God exists only in spoken words of a language."

After hearing this, the tailor bid farewell with them and departed.

And then the young man said, "And God's kingdom will arrive only when this worldwide spirit of scholasticism and verbosity and interrogation is abolished, when the questions proposed and the words spoken are only those that are pleasing to Him. All must be considered earlier before proposed in His presence."

That evening, when it was so dark that faces could not be distinguished, when all sat around the evening bonfire near the kettles, two people, a young man and an adolescent, walked up to those sitting and greeted them. They were invited to dine but the 2 declined and sat at a distance.

Then the guest young man, one of the sons of Jehovah, when they were all silent and after dinner, asked them, "Brothers, why have you arrived here?"

The older answered in true humility, "We have arrived for the sake of the God of Israel, for the sake of love. If you have something to say to us, we will be very happy, and if you do not, we would be happy just to see your face."

Love poured from his lips and an unrestrained river of life from his mouth, because love shined among them. While they were silent they communicated in an unknown language, in a language understandable only to all those born of God, to the hyssop and deep darkness and birch trees and cedars and Seraphim.

125
FINAL WORDS

I wrote all of these lines on visible paper, not for my own sake and not even for the sake of love. All of this I wrote even against my own will. But only to fulfill that obligation, to censure all of that which I had previously composed when I was on the path of unbelief and enveloped in artificiality and every deception. This will be my testimony.

I abandon all tangible books in order to accept being a part of Your book.

I consider all I have now composed as trite, as menial as the law of Moses is compared to grace. It is impossible to express the primary truths and secrets on tangible and visible paper. Enter the book of life!

Letter to the Publisher of *Scales*

The Final Address to Former Adherents.

Against Art and Science.

All that is fabricated, devised in your art, in your arts, all that could not have possibly occurred, all that is dreamed up, in the tangible world or in the imaginary – all of this I reject, and you have so much of it! True beauty is born ready with all its necessities in the heart of a person, but you are not able to wait. Your most elegant contemporary compositions I consider nothing more than intolerable.

When I read the Hebrew prophets – Habakkuk, Jonah, Micah, Ezekiel – my spirit is calm, and even with their Old Testament reprimand of arrogance, and the lack of understanding of many. But the best of your compositions are burdensome for me.

Against Your Novels.

These are nothing more than long narratives of vanity, as I call them. Why provide them with pseudonyms? What clothe them in various situations? Why compel them to speak fabrications? Why lie? The true parable is short and direct, as for example the ancient parables of the oriental sages, whose statements went over people's heads.

What you publish is applicable only to an idle society. And there is so much worthlessness, so why apply it to the theater? We should be creating a new world, a new land.

AGAINST PRESENTATIONS OR THE THEATER.

I always deeply disdained this art of presentation even when I was part of it. It was more appealing to me to read the book, rather than watch its presentation. And no matter how difficult it was to understand this, the presentation was completely opposite or modified from the book.

The theater is a school of falsity. The first liar is the actor. He laughs when he does not want to laugh, and weeps when he does not want to weep. And all the spectators are trained to accept this lie and learn to lie. This is why there is so much deceit in the contemporary educated society; it is the result of such theaters. Spectators watch the scenes as though it is real life and weep with the scenes of suffering and then overcome their tears with the next scene of something joyful. But it is all artificial. Then they return to their emaciated lives and watch it themselves as though it is also a theatrical scene, but calmly ignore the horrible events in their life.

AGAINST EDUCATION WITHOUT RELIGION
AND AGAINST ALL DEAD LIFE.

Without a church, without prayer, the most scholarly or educated person, the most kind-hearted person, will often display himself lower than the more uncultured pagan in life.

Life is as difficult for me as death is. All of you occupy yourselves only with your body and intellect, while you have no concept of spirit. You do not even know your own spirit, while God's Spirit is hidden from you.

All of your books, all of your arts, all of your sciences, all of your education, all of your cities and customs – are just one large desert.

Who of you has seen the fiery chariot of the Cherubim, which the ancients even saw?

DEFENSE OF ONLY MUSIC AND SONG.

Of all of your arts, in part I only understand and acknowledge only one, and that is what applies to church – music and song. But it is not the contemporary music and not the contemporary song. These are enigmatic sounds that are closer to occupying the fullness of the immortal and invisible world. And songs need to be displayed only from the abundance of the heart and for the edification of the Omniscient, upon the endless altar.

A Token of Memory

A Letter to My Brother by the Flesh before
His Departure to War[22]

1904

George, I am giving to you a token by which to remember me for the balance of life, for life and death, for time and further time.

How can I possibly, and just recently have I changed my ways, to teach someone or other? But just as my heart has been seriously wounded by all of my searches and with many abstentions, I see that there is no mentor. I would have been first to bend my knees and humbly accept all that proceeded from even the lowest of whomever He would send. But so I so not see this among all the nations. It is superstition and letters, or unbelief, and our deliberate reduction of His strength extinguishes His radiance. It is this just playing a game with His name, if they mix the falsity of incense and letters with His truth? If He is the consummation of the law, this signifies they do not seek to constantly hear Him, walk by His roads and His directives.

Others unconsciously are still completely full of the common arrogance of all the land and understand Him as some emaciated comprehension, as maybe just nature, or as intellect and people's conscience, but in any case, these circumcise His strength and they do not believe His secret approach. They do not believe that sooner or later He will change the entire world. No, not due to pride, but sincerely, and I never sought my own interests.

---

[22] The Russian-Japanese War of 1904-1905

I almost also declined with them. Did I not seek truth in the ceremonies, and in the letters and even among the non-believers? But truly, it was only in my humility that I searched among them also, I could not reject an unintelligible donkey, that perhaps it just might speak. It is not due to pride that I came to this conclusion, what I found. Who does not understand this, he has never seen my soul. It was not in pride, but all my mistakes occurred while in my humbleness.

But now He does not command me to reside in either pride or humiliation during my final years, but in the dignity of being one of God's sons.

George, I do not speak about myself, but I do not want you to ever reach a point of despair, so the light of belief will never extinguish before you, even on these paths of all the earth, so you know that others walk upon it, so you not go astray due to my previous departures.

This is disclosed only to those who do not have unbelief in Him.

And let me perish, but I will seek Him even to death, in the abyss and the abysses. But He has already held me by my right hand, He already dictated to me many of His commandments – and the small and great and smallest and the endless. Salvation to God!

This is a token of my memory, George, now if you will accept it. Spend time in solitude each day; when you are alone, close your windows and doors and call unto Him, the Beloved of your soul. He is the light, spouse, redemption. If you will cease worrying and arise to ask of Him of many matters, He will direct you to all. Constantly live and walk with the brethren, participants of the royal world. And the rocks and waters and plants are filled with life, and Angels continually surround all of us, and even more does He reside among His small children.

When you will preserve the dignity of your strength, when you will surely hate the flesh and not submit to it, but dominate over it like over a younger brother, then only will you bring hope to others. You will conclude a union even with the contemptible and with unfortunate, with every rock, and all these items will penetrate your heart.

Do not walk by the corporeal, but by the spirit, and compel the flesh to joyfully walk on the paths of spirit.

If you should have visions of me in the night or during the day, know that I have reached close to you, and do not think that this is just a dream, because this is your greatest strength. Be always immaculate and you will always reside with all, and will always clearly recognize those who come to you, and will always greet all friends, and they will rejoice over you. So will the transformation of the universe arrive, so will you see the beginning of complete immortality even here.

To Leo Tolstoy and his Followers

I cannot hide, I want to explain my chief differences with you.

The human spirit is not God, it is not the Father, it is only a son, it is not without a beginning, but it is immortal and endless. As the Father is without a beginning, so the son is without an end, in this manner he is like the Father. Only the Sole One is without a beginning.

This is a great secret: He was and there was no time when He did not exist. Although we use human language of a tangible and corporeal era, and every word is humanly derived, then every earthly thought is only similar or approaching what we want.

He was and there was no time when He did not exist, and He summoned all to immortal life, worldwide, for the sake of love. Not one emaciated leaf will perish. He created every blade of grass to be immortal, every grain of sand will come aflame like the sun and be transformed in Your kingdom.

The human spirit was created. In reality it was created before the entire visible world, but it was summoned to life before the beginning of time. He was always existent and will be always. Is there a better way to explain this in a human language?

This is why an abyss and the light reside in a person, he can live in complete darkness, can live in inexpressible light. In the depths of the human spirit there is a portion or spark of the eternal fire, but it is tied with the human spirit only in the manner that a bride is tied with the groom.

I strive to speak not in the language of the sons of God, but according to human contemplation, although your language is difficult. The language of a child is the language of human intellect, while the language of the sons of God is the language of worldwide love, the language worldwide endless compassion and indescribable omnipotence. For it there is no need of another science, other than purity.

My second accusation. You and Tolstoy prohibit many from researching the invisible world, the end of the world, all the secrets. You want to be liberated from contemporary non-believing society, from the poison of the non-believing system of education, but you are not liberated. The yeast of materialism is just returning to you, the yeast of coarse positive thinking.

I heard from you, brother Leo, the ancient role of dead schools: We must contemplate with the least amount of expended effort, it is enough to just know that God exists. So does this mean we need to discard all belief, that it is sufficient to love people without God?

No, brethren! Do not hold back effort while on the eternal road. Yes, even sufficient belief is unattainable for contemplation.

Of course, we need to start at the foot of the mountain in order to climb it, but not to just stamp our feet at its foot. Many secrets are also located in the book of conscience, but this is just the A-B-C's. Of course, many wanted to read the book of life, having discarded the boring and long task of learning the A-B-C's, but this was foolish. And it is also destructive to fear proceeding further than the fundamentals.

That you clearly explained that many laws of conscience definitely apply to delusional contemporary educated people (although not all of them), this is to your merit. But that many err when reading the *Invisible Book* indicates its great difficulty. Without the book of conscience you will not read the balance of books of life. Many strongly err in the former, as you know, is just acknowledging and applying the laws of conscience.

The book of life is mysterious and more difficult than the book of conscience.

But we do not want to only be children, we want to preach wisdom. The wisdom we preach is among the adults, but it is not the wisdom of this era and not derived from the authorities of this era who are just passing through, and not of the kings with their human intellect, and not derived from contemporary scholars, and not evolving from unenlightened sages.

The third of my chief accusations is that I believe in communication with the invisible world. I do not just believe, I know. I see, and not just myself, but many, even all. Of course, the approach of spirits to a human is not so ostensibly formidable, as nations feel, but it does occur. Seek the eternal truth. Flee contemporary prejudices of unbelief as well as the prejudices of superstition.

Tell the Lord, "Lord, tell me the path and I will travel it." Only then will you enter it.

He is the wisest of all.

Other than this, many of your adherents reject the especial mystic approach of the Lord to a person.

Woe not only to him who will add to the *Invisible Book*, but to him who will delete from it.

Our world, this world, either adds or deletes or rejects. This is the reason it cannot gain a victory or immortality. But all will be fulfilled.

To my Deceased Friend, Yakov Esaakovich Erlich

I saw you as I was finishing the final pages of this book. From what world were your eyes and your voice transmitted to me? I know. If you were still alive you could be the sole individual among the people of our contemporary education who would understand all my words in this book and not at the same time laugh at them. What breadth and width always resided in you. It is not due to the noble Jewish blood in you, and which is so disdained in the present nations? And because this blood was always near to the Spirit of belief. With your knowledge you did not yield to them and not one word of profanity or pride or self-interest resided in you. Because your word was much deeper and pristine than the intellect of many kings, but it was due to your knowledge that you aspired more to the immensity of the Secret. You reverently learned all you could and know all the principles and path of secular science, and not due to haughtiness, but based on truth, and you placed all of this as a footstool to Belief and Mystery, just as the body is at the feet of Spirit.

Peace be unto you. In the middle of our idle childhood and deceptive entrance into life, your along completed the imperceptible task and died as a martyr of all life.

Lord, remember him in Your eternal mind, and allow him to rise high and without an end upon Your eternal ladder.

Brethren, during life, during life do all due to love, so that great compassion will defeat it with its light at the moment of death.

LETTER TO SISTER TATYANA MIKHAILOVNA

AUGUST 24, 1940

Greetings to you from my depths, sister Tatyana and to you brother Nikolai Yuzkov,[23] to all the brothers and sisters, those with whom we shared the same one road.

I want to relate to you some of my primary issues, about my inner persuasions. I do not deny my previous paths, I do not deny their direction. Every road close to those paths, are valuable to me even at the present. Of course, what was in the old roads that I recognized as excessively superficial or ritualistic I discarded. For ages people have been tie by rituals, while ourselves, rejecting all rituals, we have been defeated anew from the side and imperceptibly.

I recognize our religious community and right now, but not strictly ostensively. Every person who approaches all goodness is already part of.

But one item that was formerly precious to me, I have finally discarded, or maybe I did not discard it, but only began to view it from another aspect.

I have abandoned all cognizance of a higher entity that is higher than a person's individuality. Even the most spiritual of such comprehensions seems to me one of the views of religious or psychological slavery. Even the smallest approach to this thought was difficult for me and seemed to be causing us to go astray. The light which I sensed clearly with my inner gaze,

---

[23] actually his brother-in-law.

169

which I accepted as the light of some special entity, was the light of my individuality.

I lived these questions to their depths, weighed them, and this question seemed excessively easy or infantile, that is, the God that I recognize is only the concept of goodness. Any other recognition was slavery for me.

I do not want to hide this from you. I declare to you the decision of my thoughts.

Of course, every laugh or ridicule at me for what I was not able to attain is just alien to me, or just plain shameful. But this is not treachery, but the conclusion of my accounts is precious to me. It is superstition that is horrible and shameful, and these ancient delusions always seem to rear their heads under thousands of new masquerades.

I grasp your hands, all those whom I have known and do presently know. Your well-known friend and brother of all worldwide communities of all persuasions.

Aleksandr Dobrolubov

Printed in the USA
CPSIA information can be obtained
at www.ICGtesting.com
LVHW092250170124
769269LV00034B/487